ZEPPELINS

ZEPPELINS

OF WORLD WAR I

WILBUR CROSS

BARNES
&NOBLE
BOOKS
NEW YORK

This edition published by Barnes & Noble, Inc.,
by arrangement with Paragon House.

1993 Barnes & Noble Books

ISBN 1-56619-390-7

Printed and bound in the United States of America

M 9 8 7 6 5 4 3 2

Dedicated to the late Captain Hans von Schiller who, over a period of several years, contributed many documents, photographs, and personal reminiscences to the author and who was a friend and colleague to most of the airship commanders and pioneers mentioned in this book.

CONTENTS

*Z*eppelins *of World War I* tells the story of the little-known aerial battles that took place over England during the Great War. In this conflict, like World War II, the Germans tried to demoralize the British by dropping tons of bombs on unprotected cities and critical industrial plants.

The book begins with accounts of the design and development of zeppelins during the prewar years and tells of their conversion from peacetime transportation use to terrifying weapons of war. Their initial bombing deployment almost paralyzed Great Britain, which at that time had no way of predicting when or where the aircraft would arrive in its nighttime skies. Even when the

British first detected the airships, they had no planes or artillery capable of reaching the enemy craft which cruised at great altitudes methodically selecting targets at will.

At the onset the first aerial battle for Britain was totally one-sided. Only serious disagreements within the German high command that stalled the development of their airships and weakened their strategic use kept England from being devastated. We then see the British respond, with ingenuity and gallantry, learning more about the nature of their enemy, setting up defenses, and perfecting fighter planes that could attain sufficient altitude to engage the giants in combat.

Rather than writing a traditional chronological history of the zeppelin in combat, I have chosen to bring the action closer to the reader by dramatizing a series of episodes characteristic of the battles that took place. I introduce the German airship commanders and pioneers who made zeppelin attacks the threat that they were to become, as well as the British gunners, airmen, and civilian volunteers who were trying to defend their homeland.

Beyond the thrilling first-person accounts of combat, the story of this unique segment of aviation history raises some interesting questions. Did the rigid airships invented by the Germans wreak the same havoc as the deadly U-boats that prowled the seas? Did the zeppelin change the nature of attack and defense in future wars? Did the rapid development and improvement of the zeppelin in a period of less than four years of war produce a means of aerial transportation that would revolutionize the aviation industry in peacetime? These and other questions are ultimately answered as accounts proceed through the war and to the aftermath, when the largest airborne machines ever created unsuccessfully sought to establish themselves as both complements of naval fleets and an advanced mode of travel and commerce.

CHAPTER 1

THE BEGINNINGS

T he man toward whom all eyes were turned was a husky sixty-two-year-old former cavalry offi cer with a white walrus mustache, an ample, slightly red nose, dark piercing eyes, and white hair mostly obscured by a white yachting cap. The place was the picturesque town of Manzell on the German side of Lake Constance. During a hot weekend in July some fifteen thousand onlookers had gathered along the waterfront and in a large flotilla of small boats, private yachts, and the commercial passenger steamers and launches that regularly plied the waters of the forty-two-mile-long Bodensee, shared by Germany, Austria, and Switzerland.

On this day, after two frustrating postponements due to high winds, Count Ferdinand von Zeppelin announced that he would finally be going aloft in what the crowd had come to see: an enormous airship as high as a church steeple and as long as an oceangoing liner.

On the shore of the lake doors on a huge shed swung open, revealing the fabric nose of the monstrous machine firmly tied to a raft. Technically a rigid airship, the dirigible would thereafter be known simply as a zeppelin after its designer, promoter, and builder. At six-thirty on this auspicious summer evening—Monday, 2 July 1900—the count stood ramrod-erect in front of the spectators, asked for silence, and led the assembled airshipmen and handlers in prayer. The moment was charged with suspense and drama; many in the audience had come with the grim expectation that the count's virtually suicidal venture would at the very least result in a twisted pile of wreckage in the shallows of the lake.

An hour later, after the barge had been towed by a small steam tug into waters free of obstructions, Zeppelin and four crew members clambered aboard a pair of aluminum structures—called gondolas by the count—slung below the long cigar-shaped hull of the airship. In the interim they had double-checked the seventeen balloon-shaped gas cells suspended inside the aluminum framework of the ship and inflated with hydrogen, supervised the pumping of almost a thousand pounds of water ballast, warmed up the two Daimler engines, and tested the operation of the pair of small propellers attached to each.

As the spectators (including a commission of Prussian army officers sent by Kaiser Wilhelm II) could observe, the ballast had now been distributed fore and aft so carefully that the ship floated on a perfectly even keel a few feet above the long pontoon raft to which it was anchored.

"Airship ready for takeoff!" shouted Count Zeppelin.

The expectant crowd grew hushed, watching anxiously as a ground crew, led by an army captain and made up of soldiers trained in the handling of tethered observation balloons, paid out the handling lines until the ship was about 150 feet above the surface of the water. It was a glorious sight as the unique craft became "bathed," as one reporter wrote, "in a glorious sunset."

The deep, guttural voice of the count resounded again from the forward gondola as he ordered, "Let go the lines!"

A cheer went up from the crowd. Boat horns barked and ships' bells rang. But almost immediately it became apparent to the onlookers and the crew members that something had gone seriously wrong. The line handlers under the bow had responded quickly to the count's order to release the lines, but those near the stern had not heard the order and had held onto their lines until they saw that the bow men had released their hold. Only a few seconds had elapsed, yet it was enough for the airship's nose to point skyward at too sharp an angle.

Instinctively the count barked out an order to start the engines. The propellers took hold, providing initial forward motion, and he was able to trim the ship as it gained headway. Eugen Wolf, a reporter selected as the official journalist to go along on the flight, later described the event, adding that the airship, "free of every shackle, majestically floated away and the thousandfold hurrahs of the crowd echoed from the shore as she slowly made her way south. . . . Everyone realized that it was not blind chance that sent her on her way, but the highest expression of human will."

The spectators watched the aerial behemoth climb to a height estimated by a member of the Prussian army commission as more than fifteen hundred feet. History was being made, he asserted vigorously, making notes for his intended report to his superiors and the Kaiser. Unhappily, his elation was a bit premature. At the controls, Ferdinand von Zeppelin was experiencing unexpected difficulties. He had managed to lower the bow and level the craft at about eight hundred feet with an ingenious device that could wind a 250-pound lead weight forward or backward along the keel. But the mechanism had jammed, leaving the weight frozen in a position much too far forward. Consequently the bow dropped below horizontal and the surge of the engines propelled the dirigible down toward the waters of the lake. The count's next maneuver was to release water from one of the forward ballast tanks. When this barely slowed the descent, he ordered the propellers thrown into reverse, a maneuver that might have worked if one of the engines had not died.

There was no choice but to make a landing. To the count's credit, he did this with such skill, using the remaining engine and deploying ballast, that he was able to settle the craft gently onto Lake Constance near a steamer landing at the village of Immenstadt, almost four miles from where it had taken off. This first flight of the first zeppelin had lasted about twenty minutes. The reporter Wolf was exuberant in his praise, forecasting that "dirigible flight is now a reality." But he was not supported by the officers of the commission, who reversed their initial reaction and eventually reported to their commanding general that the flight they had witnessed was too short, too erratic, and too slow (barely ten miles an hour) to be meaningful and that the rigid airship was "not suitable for either military or nonmilitary purposes."

Ferdinand von Zeppelin was not deterred by the reactions of his former fellow officers or by the numerous critics who accused him of being a mad scientist. He had a combination of Prussian stubbornness, creative inventiveness, and foresight that refused to give in. He refused to consider the Lake Constance flight a failure, pointing out the kinds of design changes he could make that would prevent the problems from recurring on future flights. Within days of the July second demonstration, he was already making improvements and putting on his drawing board plans for zeppelins that would be larger, faster, and capable of carrying much heavier loads.

Zeppelin was indeed a genius. It was remarkable that he had progressed to this stage in 1900, based on his minimal experience and the general lack of scientific knowledge in those days about flight, lighter-than-air or heavier-than-air. Zeppelin's experience had been almost entirely that of a traditional German army officer. He had entered the Prussian army in 1858 at the age of twenty and served in the Seven Weeks War and the Franco-Prussian War. His first experience with flight was very limited; Zeppelin had served as an observer with the Union Army during the American Civil War and saw how tethered balloons could be used by scouts to study the enemy from aloft. Not until after he retired from the army in 1891, three decades later, could he actively devote his time to designing motor-driven airships.

Zeppelin was convinced that the rigid airship was far superior to the nonrigid designs several other inventors were experimenting with. The nonrigid type, the simplest in design, was similar to balloons in that it had no fixed internal structure. Its shape was maintained by internal gas pressure, which in turn was regulated by varying the pressure in air-filled bags called ballonets inside the elongated envelope of the airship. Nonrigids buckled easily under the weight of heavy loads or the strain of wind and rain.

Some designers were also experimenting with semirigid types that had a lightweight keel part of the way along the bottom of the ship, to which were attached the motors, gondola, and controls. But Zeppelin remained convinced that the future of the airship lay in a rigid structure, composed of a skeleton that determined the shape of the airship and a keel that ran the entire length. Since the elongated envelope required no internal pressure to hold its shape, the hydrogen gas could be contained in a series of fixed self-contained cells. Thus the airship could be much longer and more easily controlled than was possible with the nonrigid and semirigid types.

After the Lake Constance flight in 1900, the count's next big milestone was the construction and testing in 1906 of a zeppelin that maneuvered far better than the earlier model and attained a speed of thirty miles per hour. Two years later, now recognized for his success, he established the Zeppelin Foundation for the development of aerial navigation and the manufacture of airships. This was located at Friedrichshafen, a southwestern German port on the Bodensee that had the necessary industries, supplies, and skilled labor to construct aircraft.

The count was also a pioneer in the development of the internal-combustion engine, the propulsion means that made the zeppelin functional and maneuverable. He supported the work of his countryman Gottlieb Daimler (whose engines he had used on the flight in July 1900), particularly in the development of an ignition system whose flame was internal and would not ignite the highly flammable hydrogen used for buoyancy in the gasbags.

How far Zeppelin's star had ascended since his first semifailure on Lake Constance is reflected in the financing of his ambitious manufacturing venture. At seventy, having plowed a great deal of his own money into the development of airships, he suffered a tragic blow with the loss of his latest ship at Echterdingen in 1908. He was plunged into despair and would have been bankrupt had the German people not rallied to his cause. The popular public subscription that followed raised a total of seven and a half million marks to rescue him from financial ruin and to establish the Luftschiffbau Zeppelin Company, where ship after ship would be built. Some of them were commissioned by the very Prussian army command that had initially labeled zeppelins militarily useless, but the majority were delivered to the subsidiary company for commercial airship navigation at Friedrichshafen, the Deutsche Luftschiffahrts-AG, later known simply as DELAG. At the start two large hangars were built; two were added at the outset of World War I. Eventually DELAG had hangars at Frankfurt, Baden Oas, Düsseldorf, Leipzig, Potsdam, and Hamburg.

Now that the construction of zeppelins was acknowledged a serious business in which citizens and officials alike took great national pride, it quickly became clear that this was a completely new industry. Consulting engineers demonstrated that it was a mistake to try to adapt conventional automobile engines and other commercial machines, products, and materials to the development of zeppelins. Consequently, the initial airship-construction firm soon evolved into a complex organization of special related companies for the manufacture of such products as motors, propellers, gears, fabrics, aluminum frames, navigational instruments, controls, and cordage.

Those who designed and experimented with zeppelins had first to understand the scientific concept of a unique craft. An airship, unlike an airplane, maintains itself in the air by the buoyancy of the gas in its bags (in this case hydrogen), which is lighter than air. Thus a cubic yard of hydrogen was able to lift about two pounds of weight. In other words, an airship could float in the air, like a balloon, without ever using its motors. In one sense, the movement of a dirigible through the air is not flying but is comparable to the movement of a sailboat through the water.

As liquid fuel is consumed by the engines, the airship naturally becomes increasingly lighter in weight. Hence, if it is to come to the ground after a voyage, it must be restored to equilibrium—to hang motionless in the air when its engines are shut off. If it were really "lighter than air," it would shoot skyward when stopped and the ground crew, rather than holding it in place and managing its position, would be lifted with it. (This kind of accident happened on numerous occasions in the early days of the zeppelin, sometimes with tragic consequences.)

Experiments with power and propulsion of various kinds led to the development of the Maybach motor, which proved to be safe, powerful, and eventually quite dependable even under adverse weather conditions. One later zeppelin ran for eight years with only a single change in its motors. This was remarkable when there were records of flights that, within a period of eight hours, involved temperature changes of seventy degrees or more in weather that ranged from totally dry to extremely wet, with snow and sleet and the entire humidity scale thrown in for good measure.

During the last decade of his life, Ferdinand von Zeppelin enjoyed recognition in Germany as the most important pioneer in the development of the rigid airship. It was sad that, before he died in 1917 at the age of seventy-nine, he saw his peacetime dream to revolutionize travel and transportation turned into a nightmare in which his once-glorious invention became a coffin for hundreds of his compatriots and an engine of destruction for many civilian victims of the war that engulfed Europe.

DOVE OF PEACE TO HAWK OF WAR

At the beginning of September 1914 England and Germany had been at war for a month and already a strange and fearful message was being repeated throughout Europe: "England will be destroyed by fire! England will be destroyed by fire!"

The origin of this threat was a song said to have been composed by a relative of the Kaiser to boost German morale in the schools and popularize the notion that the war would be over in a matter of months and the people of the United Kingdom brought to their knees. The belief was based on the conviction that the mighty zeppelin was a powerful engine of destruction second only to the fiery wrath of Vesuvius.

For more than ten years the zeppelin had proved its worth as potentially one of the greatest modes of transportation ever devised. And since 1908 it had also been the target of a great deal of military investigation and research to determine how it could be used strategically against enemies of Germany. During the two years prior to the war, with hostilities growing ever more imminent, the pace of design and construction at DELAG was increased as rapidly as manpower and facilities could be assigned to the task of building more and larger zeppelins. It was obvious, too, that if raids were to be carried out against enemy cities, the ships would need to attain high altitudes to stay above the range of artillery fire from the ground.

The delays and setbacks were many, including the loss of two of the three airships that had been purchased by the German navy. For many months it seemed as though there was little chance that zeppelins would ever be the threat the German high command had hoped they would. But that was before the arrival of Peter Strasser.

Almost a year before the beginning of the war, on a crisp day in September 1913, the scene was the naval headquarters building in Berlin, an imposing but dark and gloomy place. To the young naval officer who strode along the hardwood floor of the hallway, which echoed to the click of his highly polished boots, the atmosphere seemed even more forbidding. Berlin was an especially trying place for a young officer (he was thirty-seven) because his superiors were constantly under tension and inclined to crack down on the slightest dereliction of duty.

Strasser gave his name brusquely to the adjutant and snapped a smart salute as he was waved inside to the senior officer. He tried to hide his nervousness but was in no way relieved by the opening statement of the commander.

"Lieutenant Strasser," he began, rising and walking to the window, "I am aware of your high qualifications up to this time . . ."

What did the man mean by that—"*up to* this time?"

"We have been well satisfied with your performance, especially in gunnery." There could be no quarrel on that score. Strasser, a dedicated professional navy man who had volunteered for aviation duty almost three years earlier, had twice won the *Kaiserpreis* for having achieved the best record of any gunnery officer in the service. Not only was the senior officer aware of these honors, but he launched into a bombastic discourse on the lieutenant's marksmanship and dedication to duty before getting to the point.

"I tell you all this," he said, narrowing his eyes and looking intently at his visitor, "because I am ordering you to a new command and I do not want you to look upon it as a setback to whatever ambitions you may have as an aviator."

During an agonizing pause Strasser envisioned himself being dispatched as an instructor to a dull recruit-training group or assigned to some remote research project.

"As you know, we lost the commanding officer of our Naval Airship Division, Lieutenant Commander Matzing, in the recent crash of the zeppelin *L-1* in the North Sea."

"Yes, sir. I knew she had gone down with all hands."

"Well, to be perfectly direct with you, Lieutenant, I am placing you in command of naval zeppelins."

Strasser could hear his jaw crack as it dropped. He opened his mouth to speak but could only stutter. Seeing his hesitation, the senior officer continued his apparently rehearsed speech. Something about the position needing a man who was "dedicated . . . courageous . . . resourceful . . . willing to work against the odds." He included, too, a short dissertation about the navy having a black mark on its record because of airship accidents and failures, criticism from the high command for low morale, and stupid jokes by army brass about the navy and its "gasbags."

By the time the commander had wound himself down Strasser had regained his composure. "Sir, it is hardly within my jurisdiction to state that a mistake has been made about my capabilities," he began, "but I have no knowledge of airships. I have never been aloft in one and, though I have been assigned to aviation duty since 1911, my experience has been with the development of ordnance for converting our observation aircraft into fighter aeroplanes. We have made some substantial progress in that respect, sir, if I may say so. But as for zeppelins, I am a complete neophyte."

Strasser could not even comprehend how his name had been drawn out of the hat. Furthermore, if the navy had really been losing respect in its battle to forge the airship division into a fighting arm of the fleet, its critics could only react negatively to the appointment of a completely inexperienced junior officer to its command. As he was about to learn, the navy did not have much choice.

"I must admit to you, Lieutenant, that I am aware of your unfamiliarity with lighter-than-air craft. I must also acknowledge, in great confidence, that the *L-1* took to the grave with it not only a highly capable commanding officer but practically all of the experienced airship men we had on active duty, including several top engineering experts. We selected you because we are certain you have the technical adaptability and flexibility to transfer your talents from one assignment to a completely different kind with great effectiveness and in the shortest possible period of time."

Thus Peter Strasser, though relatively young and with no aerial track record, was thrown into a command that was to become one of the most vital, most dangerous, and most controversial of all World War I assignments. He had a number of things going for him. He was a confirmed bachelor whose only real love was his work. He was a tough taskmaster who demanded—and got—the most out of his officers and enlisted men, not only in emergencies but on a day-to-day basis. He was a stickler for discipline, vital in an arm of the service where the slightest infractions could jeopardize men, machines, and missions. And he possessed imagination and vision.

Strasser was not a big man or particularly imposing. With a small head, eyes set wide apart, a mustache and a trim goatee, he looked less like a commanding officer than like some minor railway official. But, in addition to his other qualities and the high technical skill that had made him a gunnery expert, he possessed a determination that bordered on obsession. During the month following his promotion to the position of chief of the Naval Airship Division he drove himself like a demon possessed to learn everything there was to know about airships. He conferred often with the aging Ferdinand von Zeppelin as well as with two of the count's advisers and Germany's top aviation experts, Claudius Dornier and Ludwig Dürr, technical director of the Luftschiffbau Zeppelin Company. He also had the confidence of another airship pioneer, Hugo Eckener (who would be known in the 1930s for his command of the last great airships like the *Hindenberg* and the *Graf Zeppelin*).

Strasser's cram course paid off as he learned everything there was to know at that time about zeppelins. He could be found late at night scrambling along the catwalks of the *L-2*, the only naval airship in active service at the time, studying ways to improve battle-station procedures. He helped dismantle and reassemble the engines of the *Viktoria-Luise*, a commercial airship aboard which some naval recruits were in training. He inspected every

13

inch of the five Z-class airships that belonged to the army. And he pored through every book, report, technical document, or record he could find on the history and development of lighter-than-air craft and flight. In short, he became a walking encyclopedia of facts about this new military/technical field into which he had so suddenly been thrust.

When not committed to such education, he acted as the self-appointed promoter and spokesman for the zeppelin. One of his major communications efforts was directed at convincing stolid, old-line Admiral Alfred von Tirpitz, then in his mid-sixties, that airships had a rightful place in the German fleet. He succeeded in badgering the grudging admiral to dicker with the Reichstag for funds for a replacement for the lost *L-1* and for two more ships of the same class.

Strasser had not been associated with the Naval Airship Division for more than a month when, on 17 October 1913, he received the first of what would be many similar violent and tragic shocks during his command. He was called to the telephone at air station headquarters. The hoarse and faltering voice at the other end was that of Oberleutnant Bockholt von Buttlar, one of his most experienced officers.

"*L-2* has crashed," he said. "No . . . no survivors!"

Buttlar had been at the nearby Johannistal air base, ready to board *L-2* for a test flight, but at the last minute had been replaced by another officer. He had observed the ship as she climbed lazily, seemingly under full control, to a height of about fifteen hundred feet, her naval pennant flapping sharply at the stern in a light breeze. Suddenly he had seen one of the crewmen scrambling rapidly along the lower catwalk toward the forward engine car. There was trouble.

As Buttlar watched in horror, a long tongue of flame licked

from the forward engine back along the catwalk—obviously from leaking gasoline—and suddenly leaped upward toward the bottom of the long cigar-shaped envelope that contained the hydrogen-filled gas bags. An explosion rose like the faraway sound of thunder as the underside of *L-2* glowed with flames. Within ten seconds the entire airship was afire. The framework buckled in half and the doomed ship plunged to earth.

When Strasser arrived at the scene the debris was still smoldering. Though his face was ashen, Strasser quietly and calmly began interrogating Buttlar and other witnesses about what they had observed just before and during the explosion. Had they noticed any liquid spilling from the engine? Had there been any abrupt change in the angle of the ship or the direction of flight? Had they heard any other sound prior to the explosion?

By the time he reported to the Admiralty a few hours later he was convinced that he knew the cause. It was not a gasoline leak but a flaw in the design. The forward car had been closed off in such a way that, when hydrogen gas was devalved to help trim the ship for its designated altitude and course, some of the gas was trapped in a pocket behind the windscreen. There, mixed with just enough air to make it more flammable than normal, it had been ignited by engine-exhaust sparks. The trail of flame had been the vapor spewing out behind the engine housing, now aflame and rising toward the great hull of the zeppelin.

With proper venting and baffles to contain engine-exhaust sparks, he asserted, this kind of accident could be prevented in the future.

The *L-2* tragedy almost spelled the demise of the Naval Airship Division. Had a less determined man been in command it most surely would have marked the end of the zeppelin, at least as a military weapon. But Strasser would not give in. He pointed out accurately that the development of torpedocraft and the submarine, emerging even then as mainstays of the navy, had not been without setbacks and tragedy.

The navy agreed to proceed with the construction of zeppelins. When Strasser was asked bluntly, and not a little sarcastically, how he proposed to build his "gasbag navy" with no airships in the fleet (*L-3* would not be completed until May 1914), he replied, "I have already ordered some of my officers and men to Leipzig, where I have chartered the commercial airship *Hansa* for training."

The start of the war in August 1914 found the Naval Air Division with that one lone airship, now completed and fully tested, compared with six in service with the army, mainly manned and equipped for aerial observation rather than bombing. The imbalance was quickly reduced, however, when the army lost the *Z-6, Z-7,* and *Z-8* that summer, all shot down by shrapnel while on reconnaissance flights over Belgium and France.

"When will the military learn that you simply cannot employ airships for low-altitude observation and scouting?" Strasser had emphasized repeatedly, countering the scathing criticisms of zeppelins by top-ranking officers in all branches who urged their abandonment as weapons of war. "Leave those jobs to heavier-than-air craft, which can dart quickly, avoid ground fire, and hop almost unseen from the protective cover of trees and valleys. Zeppelins are designed to fly high, operate at night or in cloud cover, and carry payloads of bombs and incendiary devices."

"You could never break his spirit," Buttlar asserted with admiration years later. "One day he would be conferring with old Count Zeppelin and Eckener. The next he would personally be delivering reports and recommendations to the Admiralty, and talking back to the admiral at that. And at almost any time you could find him up in the sky studying engine performances at the ultimate altitude he could reach."

Strasser, whose only modern-day counterpart might have been American admiral Hyman Rickover in his campaign to promote nuclear submarines to Congress, had a unique gift for entering a room full of top brass with the odds overwhelmingly stacked against him and come out the winner. Even as members of the high command and government leaders, all the way up to the Kaiser, were talking about disbanding the Naval Airship Division, he was planning gigantic zeppelin bases. He built them at Tondern, Hage, Seddin, and (the largest of all) Nordholz, where he designed a hangar large enough to hold four airships at once that revolved so the zepps housed within could be brought out safely with their noses headed directly into the wind.

"His strategy," explained another officer who knew him well, Hans von Schiller, "was primarily to wear down resistance with a marathon progression of requests, proposals, reports, conferences, and sometimes outright demands. He was neither fazed by authority nor intimidated by committees, no matter how greatly he was outnumbered."

As a result, he was able to launch the *L-4*, *L-5*, *L-6*, *L-7*, and *L-8* before Christmas 1914. By then he had no fewer than twenty-five naval flight crews in training or already in service and a total of almost four thousand officers and men on active duty at ten bases, most of them located along the northern coast of Germany, within easy striking distance of London and other English cities.

He had also almost single-handedly been responsible for negotiating contracts with DELAG to construct no fewer than twenty-eight zeppelins of a larger, greatly improved design by mid-1915. So advanced were the Germans in their technical research and engineering skills that they were said to be five years ahead of the British, whose pitiful little fleet of fewer than ten rigid airships accomplished no more than a handful of reconnaissance missions during the entire war.

17

Even the German army, suddenly awake to the fact that zeppelins might be the giant-killers in the war against the Allies, was unable to hold a candle to the navy. The best the army air service could do was commission a dozen new ships, with no firm commitment for delivery, and establish airship bases on the Eastern and Western Fronts from the Balkans to the Baltic.

At one point Admiral Tirpitz, annoyed at Strasser's ever-increasing demands for new zeppelin contracts, referred to the Naval Airship Division chief as "slightly mad and carried away with the idea that airships are more important than battleships." He was particularly incensed because the British were devising—successfully—methods of blockading the German fleet, and Strasser did not hesitate to point out that his airships could fly "high above any blockade the British could possibly set up."

An official memorandum from the navy department in the late fall of 1914, while not mentioning how units of the fleet had been bottled up, expressed the prevalent opinion of the high command that "we must not overlook any methods at our disposal to force England to her knees."

One such method was to institute bombing raids against British targets, especially London, using high-flying zeppelins as the agents of destruction. This had been Strasser's intention from the day he took over as chief of the Naval Airship Division. But now he faced an unexpected obstacle: Kaiser Wilhelm II had blood ties to the British royal family. While he had no compunctions about waging open battle against soldiers, sailors, and military bases, he cringed at the depraved reputation he would have as a murderer within his own family when German bombs killed women, children, and other British civilians.

He finally relented under the pressure of the military and shortly after New Year's Day 1915 a telegram received by the commander of the German fleet stated that air attacks on England had received approval from the Supreme War Lord: the Kaiser himself. The orders were explicit, however, authorizing airship commanders to limit their raids to docks, military facilities, and troop encampments on the lower Thames River or the coast. No bombs would be dropped on the heart of London.

Peter Strasser was ready to seize this opportunity. He had repeatedly acknowledged that raids could not be conducted without losses of airships and personnel but said that his men were eager, morale was high, and they were ready to face death in order to defeat the enemy. Some old-line navy commanders who jealously guarded their belief that ships of the line were far superior to untested aircraft obstinately decried Strasser's plan of attack. They pointed out that the bomb-load capacity of zeppelins was small indeed compared with the explosive forces that could be mounted by battleships bombarding coastal targets with continuing shellfire.

The chief responded to his critics that, while this was partially true, the raids would have a devastating effect on the morale of the British and that, furthermore, over a brief period of time his crews would force the enemy to deploy large detachments of men and critical armament from the front in order to protect the homeland. "We would also force a blackout of industrial plants," he added, "cutting down heavily on the production of arms and military equipment. We would become a strong factor both psychologically and materially in weakening the Allies in their own backyard."

On 19 January the historic event took place—the first zeppelin raid on England. An earlier attempt on the thirteenth had been frustrated by rain and fog. By this time meteorological stations had been established from the Flemish coast to Königsberg for the transmission of weather reports every three hours to a central relay station at Wilhelmshafen. The weather on the day of the raid

19

was clear at takeoff, when three new ships, *L-3*, *L-4*, and *L-6*, lifted off shortly before 11:00 A.M. The *L-6*, carrying Strasser, was plagued by engine trouble and had to turn back to Nordholz before reaching the English coast. The skies had clouded up in the afternoon and were overcast between 3:15 and 4:15 P.M., when the remaining two zeppelins had reached their target, the Norfolk region. Each one dropped six 110-pound bombs and nine incendiaries on the town of Yarmouth.

As an opener, the raid was disappointing. The bombs damaged the town square, destroyed several small buildings, killed four people, injured sixteen others, and in all accounted for less than a hundred thousand dollars in property damage.

Strasser was not discouraged. He had dramatically demonstrated that his airships could reach predetermined targets without being seriously threatened by enemy artillery fire and could deliver bombs quite accurately on selected installations. The Admiralty's announcement of the raid produced an enthusiastic response throughout Germany. An editorial in the *Kölnische Zeitung* on 21 January typified the feelings of the press on this occasion:

> . . . and now the first Zeppelin has appeared in England and has extended its fiery greetings to our enemy. It has come to pass, that which the English have long feared and repeatedly have contemplated with terror. The most modern air weapon, a triumph of German inventiveness and the sole possession of the German military, has shown itself capable of crossing the sea and carrying the war right to the sod of old England! . . . An eye for an eye and a tooth for a tooth is the only way we can treat the enemy. This is the best way to shorten the war, and thereby in the end the most humane. Today we congratulate Count Zeppelin that he has lived to see this triumph, and we

offer him thanks as a nation for having placed us in possession of so wonderful a weapon.

Less than a month later, however, the Germans received a setback when the same two zeppelins were forced down in Denmark by a gale while attempting a daring mission to bomb a British warship. Although the crews of *L-3* and *L-4* managed forced landings, the airships were assaulted by a fresh storm, torn loose despite all attempts by the crews to hold them down with ropes and weights, and blasted out to sea. They rose raggedly into the dark skies, twisted by the winds, and vanished forever, taking four crewmen with them.

This catastrophe was followed by the loss of *L-8* on 4 March when it set out for London, was struck by artillery flak near Nieuport, and forced to crash-land in Belgium. The crew had to destroy the zeppelin to prevent its capture just before surrendering themselves to Allied troops. Two days later, however, *L-9* was commissioned, followed shortly by *L-10* and *L-11*. The zeppelin construction program was in full swing. To complement the work of the engineers, an ambitious and thus-far successful training program was in progress under the able leadership of Hugo Eckener, who had been chosen by Count Zeppelin himself to head DELAG. He had helped, among other things, to oversee the construction of huge hangars at Frankfurt, Düsseldorf, Leipzig, Potsdam, and Hamburg and was probably the most knowledgeable expert in the world in the matter of airship design, construction, maintenance, operations, and training. Although Eckener was as brilliant a strategist as any zeppelin commander, he was so irreplaceable that he was forbidden by the Kaiser himself to go into combat.

Captain Hans von Schiller, one of Eckener's closest friends and colleagues in later years, spoke of the bond between Eckener and

Peter Strasser. "Hugo Eckener stood at the side of Strasser as adviser and conducted the training of the personnel. The two were bound in close friendship. Strasser was called by his first name or, at the highest court of appeal, 'God Himself.' Eckener was 'The Pope,' since he was infallible in interpreting the weather and technical questions connected with aeronautics.

"Those four years of cooperation between the two men were of enormous importance for the postwar development of zeppelin navigation. Without a Strasser, the rapid development during the war would have been impossible, and without an Eckener we would have no airships today. With an energy comparable only to that of Count Zeppelin himself, Dr. Eckener [was] able to build upon Strasser's work and, for the second time, to revive the idea of lighter-than-air navigation in spite of apparently insurmountable obstacles."

Inspired by the dedication of Count Zeppelin and Hugo Eckener, German designers and engineers were already planning airships that could carry much heavier bomb loads and range farther afield before having to return to base.

All Germany needed now was one big, successful raid to launch its basic objective to paralyze the enemy and force it quickly into submission.

CHAPTER 3

ATTACK!

15 June 1915 marks a glorious date in the annals of the Naval Airship Division. *L-10* and *L-11* were scheduled to head for the heart of England, but *L-11* had to turn back shortly after takeoff because of a broken crankshaft between the engine and the propellers, a problem that had plagued zeppelin engineers for a long time. *L-10*, however, continued on its intended course under the command of Kapitän-leutnant* Klaus Hirsch to the vicinity of the river Tyne in

---

* A rank equivalent to that of lieutenant commander in the American navy and the one to which most German airship captains were promoted.

northeastern England. That night it bombed Wallsend's Marine Engineering Works on the Tyne, the Palmer Works at Jarrow, and Cookson's Antimony Works and Pochin's Chemical Works at Willington, all of which were engaged in the production of war materials. A great amount of damage was done; seventeen workmen were killed and seventy-two were injured. The glare of the fires was visible from thirty miles out at sea on a clear, moonless night of the type airship commanders considered ideal for raids.

Strasser complimented his young commander, Hirsch, on his flawless navigation and strict adherence to a predetermined route and schedule. By this time Strasser and his staff had meticulously established a fundamental pattern for raids on Britain, taking into account all vital factors—prevailing winds, weather, the enemy's defensive artillery positions, and alternate routes to safety in the event of engine failure or other mechanical problems, sudden shifts in the weather, or unforeseen threats from enemy warships, ground fire, or aircraft.

Timing was all-important. The raids were invariably scheduled so the raiders would arrive over the target area at night in the dark of the moon—a period extending from eight days before the new moon to eight days after. This meant that liftoff times were late morning or early afternoon so the navigators could count on making a landfall over the English coast about dusk, providing a final opportunity to get their bearings before heading inland to the intended target. After arriving over their objectives in the darkest hours of the night, when they were least visible from below or from enemy observation balloons, they had plenty of time to drop their bomb loads and be well on their way back to Germany before dawn.

During the first raids the German aviators found themselves in luck because they could often navigate easily on course by following lights along roads and rivers and they often found the target gloriously lighted, just waiting to receive bomb loads. Very quickly, however, the British incorporated a system of blackouts so that the countryside, as well as the cities, could be completely darkened as soon as zeppelins were sighted or their engines detected on the crude earphones rigged up along the coast. The Germans countered by equipping their airships with flares to light up broad expanses of terrain. However, their use was spotty, often a hit-or-miss operation, and was effective only if a raider was able to get within a mile or two of the target area.

On a number of occasions the Germans attempted daylight raids when the meteorological stations predicted heavy cloud cover over England. But the reports were not always reliable and even when they were, navigators aboard ship often became confused by errors of drift, lack of instruments to measure the strength and direction of the wind, and other variables that could not be accounted for.

Airship commanders returning to base frequently found themselves embarrassed by their inability to report accurately just where they had been or what targets they had bombed. On one occasion, a new commander, described later as "a dashing twenty-six-year-old Hessian baron," maneuvered the L-6 over an English city around midnight. Despite the fact that a few ground lights were on, neither the commander nor his fellow officers could identify their position. While they were poring over their charts, trying to pick out land or water features in the darkness below, they were suddenly caught in the glare of searchlights and hit by ground fire that riddled three of the gas cells but fortunately caused no flames.

"Bombs away!" shouted the lieutenant, ordering the helmsman to swing 180 degrees and the chief engineer to bring his engines to full throttle as soon as the last 110-pounder had been jettisoned.

The next morning, safely back at the base near Hamburg, he was asked to report. He stalled for time, hoping that data recorded on the return trip might reveal something about his probable location, but no such luck. Later that day, while he was agonizing over his report, an orderly brought him a copy of the *Zeitung*. Lo and behold, it carried an announcement of the raid along with an extract from a Dutch newspaper report that German airships had struck an English town named Maldon in Essex, on the east coast Blackwater estuary. The home of iron foundries and other industries, Maldon was a prime target for raids. The lieutenant rushed his report through to headquarters and was later commended for "the accurate navigation of the airship and praiseworthy choice of a key industrial objective."

During the first raids on England, British defense commanders were greatly concerned at the manner in which zeppelins appeared able to avoid antiaircraft fire and either skirt the artillery locations or fly out of range above them. Strasser himself was greatly encouraged, in fact, when he received an intelligence report that the British were worried about their defensive capabilities and had formed a special commission to look into the problem. As he foresaw, the defense of Great Britain would at the very least be an enormous drain on English manpower and resources even if they did become effective enough to destroy some of his zeppelins in the air during strategic raids.

So vital was England's concern that it became the primary duty of the First Lord of the Admiralty, Winston Churchill, to combat the zeppelin menace. He was a formidable opponent because, in addition to making plans to strengthen and tighten the defense network, he was a proponent of the strategy that the best defense is a good offense. Putting his belief into action, he was largely responsible for a series of airplane raids against zeppelin bases that managed to destroy or immobilize at least five German airships on the ground and partially impair the airship construction schedule. One raid was notable in piercing the German defense to strike all the way to the heart of Friedrichshafen, which had been considered virtually impregnable.

Furthermore, Churchill established a branch of the Royal Naval Air Service at Dunkirk, France, on the North Sea, with a squadron of seaplanes that could deter German airship missions anywhere within a hundred miles of this base.

In part because of this strategy of attack against the German homeland, the Kaiser began to relax his initial stipulation that zeppelins must not be sent on missions over London itself In early May Strasser had interpreted orders from the high command to mean that he was now at liberty to designate London a target area. It was understood, of course, that airship commanders were to take great care to aim their bombs at industrial plants, naval shipyards, army encampments, and other military sites and scrupulously avoid harm to civilians. But no one knew better than Strasser that aerial bombing had not yet reached a precision where such selective targeting was practical or even possible.

Ironically enough, it was not one of Strasser's L-class ships, but an army airship, the *LZ-38*, that showered the first bombs on London. The attack occurred in the late spring when army captain Erich Linnarz navigated his ship over the heart of the city on 31 May.

"London was all lit up and we enjoyed total surprise," Linnarz would write in his report, telling how unsuspecting the British were that such an attack could be possible. "Not a searchlight or antiaircraft gun was aimed at us before the first bomb was dropped." So skillful was his approach that he was able to remain over the city for more than ten minutes while releasing more than 150 bombs and incendiaries. He inflicted severe damage in certain areas and killed or wounded forty-two people, most of them civilians.

Churchill exacted his revenge barely a week later when his special naval aviation unit dispatched two flying boats to the German base and destroyed the *LZ-38* on the ground.

On 9 August Strasser tested a new strategy: the mass raid. The idea was that, though British defense might be somewhat effective against a lone zeppelin or even two, its searchlight crews and antiaircraft battalions could not hope to cope with a whole squadron of airships. His intended target was London as he led *L-9*, *L-12*, and *L-13* from their base at Hage and *L-10* and *L-11* from Nordholz around noon that day with the expectation of being over the British capital around midnight. These were ships that ranged from 529 to 536 feet in length and had sixteen gas cells, each ship capable of lifting up to thirty-five thousand pounds in all—including engines, crew, equipment, and bombs.

The mission was ambitious but ran afoul of the weather and endless mechanical difficulties. Strasser, in *L-10*, ordered a rendezvous of all ships, after which each commander was to proceed independently on a westward attack course, drop bombs on the London docks and, if possible, the industrial part of the city, then turn north and run off to the northeast. Not one of the zepps managed to reach London that night. *L-13* turned back near the coast with engine trouble and had to dump incendiaries into the sea to lighten ship. *L-11* dropped her bomb load inadvertently into the sea when, coming under fire from naval artillery, her commander mistakenly concluded that he was over the city of Harwich. *L-10*, groping through thick rainclouds and mist, seemed to her officers to be at a position on the Thames over eastern London and thus dropped her payload. Later it was ascertained that the airship was actually over the island of Sheppey and the bombs had fallen on the landing strip of the Eastchurch Naval

SCRIBE TODAY and save up to 80% off the cover price!

BUSINESS REPLY MAIL

FIRST-CLASS MAIL   PERMIT NO. 628   PALM COAST FL

POSTAGE WILL BE PAID BY ADDRESSEE

FLYING®

PO BOX 422513
PALM COAST FL 32142-6446

NO POSTAGE
NECESSARY
IF MAILED
IN THE
UNITED STATES

SAVE 80%

COVER PRICE
$119.76

YOUR COST
$24

YOU SAVE
$95.76

☑ **Yes!** Please start my subscription to *Flying* for the term selected below:

☐ 2 years (24 issues) $24 – I save 80% off the cover price!

☐ 1 year (12 issues) $14 – I save 77% off the cover price!

Name *(please print)*

_____

Address

_____

City _____ State _____ Zip _____

E-mail Address   6408SA FLY

We will not share your email address with any third party.

☐ Payment enclosed.   ☐ Bill me.

f Find us:
facebook.com/FlyingMagazine

 Follow us:
@FlyingMagazine

Air Station, doing little damage. Although a total of 440 bombs had been carried on this ill-fated raid, only *L-9* managed to do any damage, destroying several buildings and causing a total of twenty-seven casualties at Goole, an inland port on the river Humber in northern England.

For those aboard *L-12* the mission was a constant nightmare. She actually made a good landfall at Westgate, south of the Thames, but because of the rain and fog was then judged to be far to the north on the Norfolk coast. Deciding that it was too late to reach London, her commander, Werner Peterson, decided to attack Harwich, which he viewed below as a cluster of lights marking a fortification there, but which later were identified as the harbor lights at Dover. Consequently, only three incendiaries hit the land while twenty-four other bombs and incendiaries fell harmlessly into the water.

Peterson paid dearly for his audacity when a three-inch gun in the harbor compound hit *L-12* aft with one of a dozen rounds and tore holes in two gas cells. On the intercom to the control car, the commander soon learned that the rips were too large to repair. Already he could tell that the ship was settling slowly at an ever-increasing angle despite his efforts to keep her aloft by speeding up the engines.

"Jettison all spare parts and provisions," he ordered, shortly after that adding machine guns, ammunition, and spare clothing to the list of items tossed overboard. It was apparent now that the ship could not long remain airborne.

Knowing that it was useless to try to reach the nearest zeppelin base, Peterson steered southeast for German-occupied Belgium. But even this hoped-for haven was far beyond reach. Around three in the morning the crew ripped out everything that could be pried loose, including the radio and its enclosure, fuel tanks, handrails, and parts of the now-stilled engines. Just before dawn the airship settled stern-first on the calm, misty waters of the English Channel and began drifting northward as the still-inflated parts of the bag caught a light breeze.

The officers and men had little trouble clinging to the wreckage or lying in the after gondola, which was semifloating like a boat. But for a while leaking hydrogen and gasoline fumes threatened to overpower them and several times they had to slip into the water and swim away long enough to draw in refreshing breaths of air.

Just after dawn they were sighted by a German torpedo boat, which approached at full speed. Peterson had planned to torch the remains of *L-12* should rescue seem imminent or an enemy vessel be seen to approach. However, when the torpedo boat's captain informed Peterson that they were not far from Zeebrugge, the commander decided, with typical Prussian doggedness, that he was not going to give up his ship. A hawser was made fast to the mooring ring at the bulbous nose and slowly the downed airship was towed in the direction of Ostend, where she was brought alongside one of the docks by early afternoon.

Peterson had high hopes that he could repair the damage to the upper skeleton, repair and inflate the torn gasbags, replace vital jettisoned equipment, and actually be airborne again. But the Allied forces nearby had other ideas, having soon learned that one of the raiders had fallen to the sea. Six British naval seaplanes from Churchill's Dunkirk base attacked *L-12* as she lay helpless alongside the dock. The pilots not only met heavy fire and scored no hits but saw one of their number shot down in flames as well. Peterson never did get his craft airborne, but most of the huge envelope, framework, and gas cells were dismantled and salvaged to become part of a brand-new zeppelin.

Strasser was not only undismayed by the failure to reach London but also felt that this latest sortie had provided some valuable lessons that would make future attacks more certain of success. Assembling all of the officers and key enlisted men on the mission, he pored over every phase of each ship's course and actions to determine where there were flaws, where and how things that went wrong might have gone right, and what to do to make future missions more reliable and effective.

"We are very close," he said, "to attaining a near-perfect raid on London."

He was absolutely right.

Shortly after two in the afternoon of 8 September 1915 *L-13* again lifted off the naval base at Hage, headed for London. This time her engines had been checked and rechecked to make certain there would be no recurrence of the mechanical problems that had caused her to turn back on 9 August. Furthermore, she was under the command of Kapitänleutnant Heinrich Mathy, an officer and ex-destroyer captain who had the consummate respect of everyone in the service and whom Strasser considered the most experienced and capable commander in the Naval Airship Division. Mathy was a handsome man with a rugged physique and a cool head. He was recognized widely throughout the airship service as the most experienced and skillful zeppelin commander and was deeply respected by his good friend and superior, Peter Strasser. That respect was shared by all members of his crew.

Mathy had literally grown up with lighter-than-air craft, having had experience with ballooning in his teens and early training in nonrigid airships long before the start of World War I. He had a feel for airships and what they could do and how they could be handled. He was never foolhardy, but he was daring in his strategy. On one occasion, just before setting out for a raid on England, he had ordered all machine guns and ammunition removed from his ship so that he could increase his bomb load. He preferred to be able to inflict more damage on British installations than have the protection against fighter planes that was becoming increasingly needed.

Mathy was calm, deliberate, and businesslike. But he could also be outspoken and very decisive. He, more than any other commander—even those in the German high command—was the one who most often urged Peter Strasser to refrain from going along on raids. He advocated the development of airships that could climb to greater altitudes. And he was adamant that zeppelin raids be continued, even increased, at a time when they were to be curtailed during the construction of a new fleet of higher-climbing zeppelins. The Germans had recently lost ten airships and more than 160 officers and men and it seemed strategically smart to limit operations temporarily. Even Strasser was convinced that the raid schedule should be greatly reduced. But Mathy stuck to his guns.

"You say our losses are heavy—and they are. You say we are not destroying enough targets—but we are beating the enemy in another way. We are forcing the British to maintain huge defense forces at home rather than sending them to the front lines to attack our soldiers." As a result of his strong, continuing arguments the Germans cut back the zeppelin program only slightly at that time, and then largely because of spells of bad weather.

Mathy earned a reputation, too, as a strategist. He was the one who worked out a plan whereby zeppelins would approach London (and other English cities) with the wind directly astern, for greater speed, rather than using the conventional method of zigzagging to dodge the searchlights. He also made use of an effective ruse: firing white flares, the signal used by British fighter planes when they were attacking zeppelins. When such flares were spotted by ground crews, they dimmed their searchlights and ceased artillery fire so as not to endanger the pilots.

32

Mathy had attended many of his superior's orientation sessions to determine how to utilize zeppelins to greatest advantage. Of particular value had been the most recent session, in which fellow commander Oberleutnant Friedrich Wenke had described his experience in *L-10* on a mission over London on 17 August. He had made his landfall, Orford Ness, with pinpoint accuracy and, despite a ground mist, had been able to check his course and position so that he had no difficulty heading straight for London and remaining right on line. Shortly before 11:00 P.M. he had sighted the city, marked by "a glow like an aurora on the southeast horizon."

Just before midnight, *L-10* attacked.

"Since it had turned into a clear, starry night," said Wenke, "I steered for the west end of the city so as to have the wind abaft the beam. We turned onto an easterly course and crossed the center of the city at ten thousand feet, a bit to the north of the Thames. When we were between Blackfriars and London bridges, I ordered the bomb-dropping to begin. We could soon observe huge fires and smoke and see buildings collapsing."

Of special value to Mathy were Wenke's comments that "the London searchlights cannot hold a ship at ten thousand feet in clear weather, even if they have sighted on her."

Shortly after two o'clock in the afternoon of 8 September Mathy ordered *L-13* aloft from the Hage field on the north coast of Germany with a complement of sixteen officers and men and a bomb load of slightly over four thousand pounds. When the ship reached fifteen hundred feet he steered toward Norderney, an island in the North Sea, to rendezvous with *L-9*, *L-11*, and *L-14* and set a westerly course toward England.

The weather was favorable as the ships made steady progress, each powered by four of the new Maybach CX engines, which had proved the most reliable type available for zeppelin flight. Named after Carl Maybach, the engineer who had designed it, the prototype Maybach engine had been tested by Count Zeppelin for use on his first airships. It differed from engines designed for the early airplanes in that its shaft rotated more slowly but was strong enough to power large propellers. It burned the low-octane gasoline of the era and was unique in that its spark plugs and other electrical components were shielded so that no spark could ignite hydrogen in the event of a leak from the large gasbags above.

Activity aboard the zeppelins was deceptively low-key as they formed for the raid against England. Except for lookouts located in the gondolas and atop the airships and the enginemen, the crews relaxed in hammocks slung amidships in the gangways inside the hulls.

It was 8:30 P.M. when *L-13* reached a point just off the English coast, almost an hour earlier than Mathy had intended, so he purposely hovered with his engines at idle until nine-fifteen, by which time total darkness had obliterated the sea below. Observers, however, could detect the sheen of a river and the lights of two villages ahead—points that would help guide them toward London. By this time *L-9* had swung toward the north to try to hit a chemical plant on the north coast and had long been out of sight. Mathy was concerned about *L-11* and *L-14*, which had drifted behind an hour or so earlier and seemed to be experiencing engine trouble. There was nothing he could do about that and no way he would break radio silence to find out.

As *L-13* moved inland in the black of night, Mathy slowly brought her to an altitude of seven thousand feet until he reached the city of Cambridge, some fifty-five miles north of London, which he had selected as his staging point. Not only was the river Cam a sliver of silver even in the darkness, but he was now near enough the British capital to see a glow of lights. That was very favorable for, besides aiding his ship's navigation, it indicated that the British "ears" and observers had not yet detected an enemy in the sky and would be little prepared for his attack.

L-13 moved in for the kill as the chronometer showed 11:40. Her altitude was about eight thousand feet. Her engines were set at low cruising speed to minimize any noise that might be detected by British defense stations. As the airship passed over the northwestern suburbs Mathy was astonished at how clearly he could make out certain landmarks that were as well lit that night as he remembered them from a peacetime visit to the city six years earlier. In the control car, he gave orders quietly and carefully so that his bombardier could take the most accurate aim possible. Among the 4,000 pounds of explosives on board was a monster for that era that weighed 660 pounds. He was saving that until he had released smaller bombs and incendiaries to line up his prime target—the Bank of England.

"First bombs away!" he ordered. When he saw the pattern of strikes below, he headed past the Houses of Parliament and directly toward his objective. Almost immediately lights started to dim and go out all through the city and the zeppelin was rocked by the first rounds of antiaircraft fire from the twenty-six gun batteries ringing London. None came close during the first barrage. But now, the stilettolike fingers of searchlights were probing the darkness, trying to catch and hold the airship. Mathy closed his eyes as one beam flashed by. It was more difficult now to make a sighting, so he had to use all his judgment and experience before ordering the release of the big one, followed by a shower of incendiaries and smaller bombs.

After completing his mission with great skill and a fine display of cool-headed concentration while under intense fire, Mathy ordered full speed (slightly over sixty miles per hour) and headed for home at an ever-diminishing altitude. Behind him he left 109 casualties and massive damage that, in today's money, would have amounted to more than $200 million. Even more important, he left London in a panic and the British with the sudden realization that the threat from the air was very real and that future bombing raids could be much more devastating.

The effect on the British was well documented by an American journalist, A. E. Shepherd, who happened to be in Fleet Street, in the heart of the city, that fateful night. Later he wrote his impressions as he watched in disbelief and as the London population stood dumbstruck, almost too terrorized to move, like a victim about to be attacked by a deadly snake.

Traffic is at a standstill. A million quiet cries make a subdued roar. People stand gazing into the sky from the darkened streets. Among the autumn stars floats a long, gaunt Zeppelin. It is dull yellow, the color of the harvest moon. The long fingers of searchlights, reaching up from the roof of the city, are touching all sides of the death messenger with their white tips. Great booming sounds shake the city. They are Zeppelin bombs—falling, killing, burning. Lesser noises, of shooting, are nearer at hand—the noise of aerial guns sending shrapnel into the sky.

"For God's sake, don't do that!" pleads one man to another who has just struck a match to light a cigarette.

Whispers, low voices run all through the city. As though voices could be heard aloft and another rain of fiery destruction sent to silence them.

Suddenly you realize that the biggest city in the world has become the night battlefield on which seven million harmless men, women, and children live.

Mathy's assistant engineman on the raid, one of the few old-time zeppelin survivors to outlive the war, told in his memoirs in the early 1920s what it was like to be on the other side of the historic battle:

We were at about eighty-five hundred feet when we released our 660-pounder, the largest anyone had ever dropped up to that time. It did not hit the intended target, but you could see a whole mass of structures and street paving swallowed up in a tremendous crater, even at our height. We were awestruck and frozen as we stared until all at once we realized that we were caught in the glare of what seemed like a dozen searchlights. In the bright light, I could look down and see black objects almost floating up toward us. Flak from the antiaircraft guns. Very close.

"Let's get the hell out of here!" someone shouted from the other engine gondola. I agreed. But Commander Mathy continued circling as coolly as though we were in a canoe looking for a place to have a picnic. We still had a few more bombs on board and he was going to use them. Damned but he was a great airship officer!

We dropped the rest of the load over a railroad station and had the satisfaction of seeing rails and ties and pieces of a depot and two big buses spouting into the air and then dropping back in a mass of wreckage. It was easy to see all this because we had dropped so many incendiaries and there were pools and rivers of fire all along the streets below.

By this time—thank God!—the commander appeared satisfied that we could do no more damage. He ordered us away at full speed, at the same time climbing to twelve thousand feet, where there was a flimsy smudge of clouds in an otherwise clear sky. It was a good thing because the gunners below were zeroing in on us—what a huge target we were!—and all we needed was one direct hit to go up in flames. That would have been death for all sixteen of us on board. We never carried parachutes. The policy of the High Command was to use every ounce of each Zeppelin's carrying capacity for bombs and incendiaries, not for parachutes (which in those days were heavy and bulky and often failed anyway) or amenities for the crew.

Despite the altitude and the fact that the night was cool to begin with, I realized that I was perspiring heavily just from the tension up there. It was an immense relief to hear the engine I tended humming at full speed and to see the glow of London fading astern. We hadn't been over the center of the city more than twelve or fifteen minutes in all. But it seemed like an eternity. It took us about ten hours to cruise back across the North Sea to Hage, our base. Some of the crewmen who were off duty climbed into hammocks and got some sleep. I myself was off duty half of that time, but I couldn't even take a catnap. I was too charged up by what we had done and what I had seen.

I watched the dawn come up over the horizon and I thought how glorious it was. I was never a religious person but I thanked the Lord for letting me survive. And I prayed that I could be that fortunate on the next raid. And the next. And the next. But I was resigned to my fate. All of us in the Zeppelin service were. You couldn't keep dealing cards forever without sooner or later coming up with the Black Ace!

LONDON ON ITS KNEES

The British reacted officially to the devastating raid that September night in 1915 very poorly and in secret. On the surface, the British Home Guard kept its usual stiff upper lip and emphasized to the press and anyone else who would listen that the damage from the zeppelin's bombs was largely confined to nonmilitary targets, including a city park, several commercial buildings, streets, and some textile warehouses. They pointed out that their revered St. Paul's Cathedral had been spared by a miracle when a near miss destroyed adjacent structures and that two city buses had received direct hits, during which many civilians were killed or maimed.

What the British did not say publicly appeared in a top-secret report to the Admiralty, a document that provided the German high command with a glorious burst of satisfaction when one of its Britain-based spies managed to obtain and forward a copy to Berlin. It was long, circuitous, and extremely detailed. But, in brief, the points made by the official military report were:

- A lone enemy aircraft had, within the space of one quarter of an hour, inflicted more damage and casualties on the British than most enemy actions had been able to do in campaigns lasting for many days or weeks.
- The attack was a total surprise, finding the Home Guard unaware of any danger until the first bomb exploded on British soil.
- Searchlight crews beamed their lights on the airship haphazardly and were unable to hold them in focus for more than a few seconds at a time.
- Antiaircraft guns could not get the range or anticipate the movement of the zeppelin effectively despite the fact that gunnery officers had at least fifteen minutes in which to aim and make a hit.
- British aircraft could not come to the defense because the planes were not equipped for night fighting and even in daylight would have had difficulty climbing to that altitude in time to attack.
- A raid by two or more airships would have logically multiplied the damage greatly and, more importantly, would have caused great confusion among searchlight and gunnery crews.
- It could be expected with total certainty that the Germans would become increasingly effective in raids on British cities as they scheduled mass attacks, improved the effectiveness of bombing instruments, developed airships that could carry larger payloads, and increased their high-altitude capabilities.

The commander of the Naval Airship Division, who was naturally on the list of top-ranking German officers to receive a copy of the report, was overjoyed to learn of England's distress. Although it was not spelled out in so many words, Peter Strasser could read between the lines that the enemy was greatly concerned about the enormity of the situation that would be imposed by repeated zeppelin raids: Even though the defense of England could be made more effective and could keep pace with technological improvements by the Germans, the British would have to commit massive sums of money, new equipment, and manpower to counter the increasing threat. As a consequence there would be fewer troops and less armament to send to the Allied front.

For the British, World War I was barely a year old when, in the fall of 1915, the Home Guard evaluated the effect of zeppelin raids, an almost totally unexpected form of warfare that threatened the nation. From mid-January until mid-October, when weather forced a seasonal halt to aerial warfare, German airships completed twenty-two raids, mainly against London and its suburbs. In all, 208 people were reported killed and more than 530 wounded. Damage was generally minimal, except for two raids on September eighth and ninth, which left 165 casualties and started large fires in the heart of London.

Nor were the Allies faring well in the front lines. During the winter a French drive had been repulsed in the Battle of Soissons on the Aisne River in northern France. In March the British had sent a naval force to occupy the Dardanelles, a strategic strait off Turkey, and take Constantinople but had failed. In April the Germans had introduced another unexpectedly terrifying threat, releasing poison gas during the second battle of Ypres in southwestern Belgium, near the French border. Greenish-yellow clouds rolled forward over five miles of the front, transfixing soldiers who did not know what they were until it was too late. Hundreds choked to death in the deadly chlorine.

On 7 May 1915 the British liner *Lusitania* was sunk by a

German U-boat, with a loss of 1,195 passengers and crew. Although this was a great tragedy for the British, the fact that 128 U.S. citizens also died was a big factor in swaying opinion against the Germans and ultimately resulting in America's decision to fight against them. In June the Germans launched a major offensive in the Argonne.* The terrain, nicknamed the Meat Grinder, had been turned into a labyrinth of barbed wire, steel barriers, muddy trenches, and concrete blockhouses—the epitome of the horrors of infantry warfare.

By August the Germans were entering Warsaw and pushing the Russians back in such disarray and with such heavy losses that they barely escaped being encircled. An Allied moment of hope that year had come when the Italians declared war on Austria. It was dashed when the Italians lost the battle of Isonzo on its northern frontier, the first of eleven losing engagements that would claim a quarter of a million Italian casualties before the end of the war.

The British suffered two naval setbacks in the Dardanelles in 1915. The overall Allied gloom was somewhat lightened when the great Russian withdrawal from Poland finally came to an end and British forces ousted the Germans from their newly acquired territory in Southwest Africa. But the British were certainly not happy about their home front during this period and the fact that what one artillery captain described as "a handful of suicidal aeronauts in flying sausages" was tying the hands of so many troops and so much equipment far, far from the front lines.

The officers and crews of the zeppelins, at first dismayed that their raids had not inflicted more damage on military and indus-

---

* Columbia Encyclopedia describes it as "a region of the Paris basin, NE France, in Champagne and Lorraine . . . a hilly and woody district centering around the capital, Saint-Menehould."

trial targets, gradually became aware that they were accomplishing an even more strategic mission by hog-tying the enemy at home. So it was a double triumph for the Germans on those occasions when their bombs were effective, as they had been on the recent raid.

Following that raid Strasser was commended by Admiral Georg von Müller, chief of the Emperor's naval cabinet, for a job well done and for following the Kaiser's directive that no bombs be dropped near Buckingham Palace or venerable historical buildings. Mathy's accomplishment that night and the news of the British reaction did much to elevate Strasser's spirits. Moreover, he needed a boost to his personal morale. Not long before receiving the British report he had witnessed a very horrifying scene. On the coast of the Helgoländer Bucht near Cuxhaven he had been observing *L-10* heading for a landing at her base in Nordholtz. He saw the zeppelin approaching at about two thousand feet in stormy skies. She was under the command of the same Oberleutnant Friedrich Wenke who had provided Mathy valuable information about London searchlights and antiaircraft emplacements.

As Strasser watched, he saw the 540-foot-long airship making a turn over Neuwerk, a small offshore island, ready to head for the field. At that instant there was a brilliant flash of light and within seconds *L-10* was enveloped in flames. Had she been struck by lightning? Had an electrical charge in the atmosphere touched off the hydrogen? No one ever knew. The only certainty was that nineteen experienced zeppelin men, including her commander, were lost in the crash. There were no survivors.

Strasser personally investigated every aspect of the accident, to determine what had to be done to prevent any recurrence of such a tragedy. He conferred with observers in the coastal batteries near Cuxhaven and it was generally agreed that the airship had been partially hidden in a cloud bank at the time and could have been struck by a bolt of lightning. She had fallen on a sandbar near the island and the captain of a picket boat reported seeing "two men leaping from the falling ship into the water." By the time he had sped to the scene, however, the wreckage lay in about ten feet of water and there was no sign of life.

After studying the firsthand accounts, Strasser dictated a memo to all of his airship commanders. In it he emphasized that great caution had to be taken when maneuvering from one altitude to another. It was vital that gas be valved off when necessary so that the internal pressure in each gasbag never exceeded a certain critical level. What could happen (and what he decided had happened in the case of *L-10*) was that the air pressure could exceed the safe limit and thus produce static electricity that would ignite leaking hydrogen. Such pressure build-ups also occurred in cases where ships were forced to fly through thunderheads, even though they might not be endangered by lightning.

Tragedy was by now a constant companion of the man who was becoming affectionately known by his officers and men as "God Himself," yet each death and each ship destroyed was a wrenching personal loss. Strasser had welded his initial tiny group of airship pioneers into an elite corps of the finest, most dedicated officers in the entire German navy. They were said to have more elan, more spirit, more daring than even the much-touted submarine commanders who put to sea in their "iron coffins," often never to return. Most were volunteers, young men whose devotion to airships and to their commander exceeded that of any other arm of the military. Their dedication was all the more impressive in view of the fact that Strasser demanded the closest attention to detail, was quick to reprimand even the most minor infraction of rules, and simply assumed that every officer under his command was imbued with great initiative and technical capability.

During off-duty hours, however, Strasser habitually joined his subordinates in drinking and partying, all but shedding his rank and usually ending up paying for these affairs out of his own pocket. A bachelor, he had no family commitments; his officers became his only "family" and he was grief-stricken when one of them died in the line of duty.

One of the biggest problems Strasser and his superiors faced was maintaining morale during the lulls between raids, especially when continuing bad weather and winter conditions kept the airships grounded for many weeks at a time. Recreational and sports facilities were very limited, mainly because of tight wartime budgets and lack of supervisory personnel. All airship commanders were expected to institute rigid, in-depth training programs for their crews as well as to become themselves familiar with technological developments and improvements in mission strategy. But zeppelins were relatively uncomplicated machines, using controls that were simple if not crude. Their internal-combustion engines were only a step removed from the ones that powered motor lorries of the day. Their armament was such that the handling of machine guns, flares, bombs, and bombsights could be mastered even by a novice in a matter of two or three weeks.

Much of the officers' spare time was spent poring over maps and charts and blurry aerial photographs so that they could familiarize themselves in as much detail as possible about the enemy territory over which they would be flying and the targets at which they would be aiming. Considerable attention was given to meteorological studies and reports to help them anticipate abrupt or uncharacteristic changes in the weather in the North Sea and over the terrain of southeastern England. These, too, were rudimentary, since even the most accomplished meteorologists of the day lacked the knowledge and instrumentation to do more than make educated guesses as to what the weather would do at any time or in any zone.

The German high command tried to reduce monotony and improve morale through interservice programs that would occupy the time of officers and men alike. For the most part, this activity consisted of collaboration with the imperial navy on fleet maneuvers in which zeppelins were used for observation and scouting. Some pioneering attempts were made to drop bombs on towed targets at sea, but these were quickly abandoned. It was realized early on that zeppelins would have to cruise so high beyond the reach of naval vessels below that they could not possibly strike ships with any degree of accuracy.

Inactivity was particularly tough on men of the type and caliber of the officers who had volunteered for duty in the zeppelin service. Most of them were unmarried and ranged in age from their mid-twenties to early thirties. There was Heinrich Mathy, who could somehow return from a twenty-four-hour raid looking as fresh and clean-shaven as though he were getting ready for a date; the steady, dependable Bockholt von Buttlar; the handsome, blond Joachim Breithaupt, who looked like a college boy; the heavy-set Prussian Alois Böcker, who would have seemed at home on the bridge of a battleship; Mathy's second-in-command, Victor Schütze; Adjutant Peter Wendt, who relieved his superior of endless reports and paperwork; Max Dietrich and Martin Dietrich, both accomplished engineers; and a new officer named Werner Peterson, an incurable romantic—a poet who liked to quote lines about ancient airborne heroes like Icarus and Daedalus.

Then there was young Kapitänleutnant Odo Loewe, skipper of a new ship, *L-19*, who was soon to meet an ironic end, with the difference between life and death for him and his entire crew a matter of only a fifty-foot swim. Strasser had been leading a mass raid over the English Midlands on 31 January 1916. When he reached base, after twenty-two hours in the air, he immediately began to check the return of the nine ships that had been with him. Only one was missing—*L-19*. Through the long hours that followed he questioned the other commanders and waited, waited, waited.

"When did you last see Loewe?"

"What was *L-19*'s position as she separated from you?"

"Was there any indication that she had been hit by AA fire at any time?"

"Did anyone pick up radio signals during the night?"

As time ran out and the days passed, *L-19* was given up for lost "somewhere in the North Sea." Had she fallen on British soil or any other land, intelligence reports would have by now revealed the presence of wreckage.

Two weeks went by before there was any clue. Then a German fisherman found a bottle floating in the North Sea. Inside was a message:

With 15 men on platform of *L-19*. Longitude 3° East. The envelope is floating without any car. I am trying to send the last report. We had three engine breakdowns. A very high headwind on the homeward flight hampered progress and drove us in the fog over Holland when we came under rifle fire. Three engines failed simultaneously. Our position becomes increasingly untenable. Now about one o'clock in the afternoon. Our last hour is approaching. Loewe.

The full account remained a mystery to the Germans for many months. Then the complete story surfaced by way of intelligence agents in Switzerland (part of an information network Strasser had ingeniously and doggedly established over numerous objections from top brass). Shortly after crash-landing in the North Sea, *L-19* was spotted, broken in half but still afloat, by a small British fishing trawler, the *King Stephen,* 120 miles east of the Spurn lightvessel that guided ships entering England's river Humber past Spurn Head. The German commander and fifteen other members of the airship's complement were clearly seen atop the still-floating bag of the zeppelin as the trawler navigated to within fifty feet of the wreckage.

Since one of *L-19*'s officers spoke English, words were easily exchanged as Loewe requested that he and his men be taken aboard, swimming that short distance if the British were worried that the trawler's propeller would become entangled in the fabric or loose ropes. Then, to the dismay and astonishment of the Germans, the *King Stephen* backed off and made a beeline at full speed to the west. It was later reported that her captain had become suddenly fearful that the raiders would overpower his crew, seize the vessel, and head for the German shore.

By the time he had located a British warship and reported his discovery, *L-19* had sunk and all of the survivors had drowned.

The records of such disasters are interspersed with some strange and remarkable escapes from death by airship crews. One of the most bizarre occurred when an army ship, the *SL-2*, returned from London after making a successful raid against four strategic shipping docks. *SL-2* was not specifically a zeppelin, but the product of the Schütte-Lanze factory (hence the *SL* designation), several years old and newly rebuilt. With only one of her four engines still functioning, she had to crash-land before reaching an intended base near Brussels. She fell directly atop a small house whose roof penetrated the hull. Although a fire was burning in the hearth inside the house at the time of the accident, the ship did not catch fire and explode. As it turned out, the chimney projected upward between two gas shells, and all the heat and smoke was carried into the open air rather than into the hull.

Much later, the zeppelin *L-33* was struck squarely amidships by an artillery shell during a raid on London. To make matters worse, the shell exploded inside the hull, tearing open several of the gas cells. Yet no fire resulted. *L-33* eventually had to crash-land not far away. The Germans tried to set fire to the ship before the British could arrive and capture it along with them. But the zeppelin refused to ignite and the enemy had itself a fine big prize of war.

In numerous other cases crews escaped just when a fiery death seemed inevitable.

One of the most famous zeppelin commanders in the history of lighter-than-air craft, Hans von Schiller, explained how and why such "miracles" could occur on these occasions. "I have to make one important point about the supposed flammability of a hydrogen-filled airship," he said. "Hydrogen alone does not burn and only when mixed with oxygen does it become dangerous. If you fill a test tube with hydrogen, invert it so the gas will not escape, and insert a burning match, the latter will go out immediately. It takes fire again when removed since there is a mixture of hydrogen and air at the mouth of the tube. The scientific principle involved in this experiment is equally valid on a large scale."

Even lightning, he added, is by no means so great a danger as one might imagine. He cited the time the *L-11* was caught in a violent storm. She was struck by lightning many times, mostly on the nose, where it was later found that the metal framework had actually been fused by the heat.

"The framework of the ship offered such a large metal surface," Schiller explained, "that no further damage was done and the electric charges left the ship immediately through the exhaust of the engines, which consisted of pure water vapor. It would have been dangerous only if hydrogen gas were blown off in or near a storm." For that reason, airship commanders and their crews had it drummed into them that they must never, never valve off gas in a storm.

Another near-tragedy and escape from death occurred to Heinrich Mathy himself when he attempted a repeat performance of his highly successful lone raid on the British capital. Less than a week after his London debut Mathy was ordered to lead a three-ship raid, again in *L-13*. But fate, in the guise of severe thunderstorms and headwinds, was against him. Despite the fact that the two accompanying zeppelins had to turn back before crossing the North Sea, Mathy persisted and reached the English coast a few minutes after midnight. He was by now so far behind in his intended schedule that he estimated arriving over London around 4:00 A.M., which would not give him much time for a bomb run before daylight would make him a sitting duck. He reasoned—correctly—that he might have the big advantage of surprise, since the British had seldom experienced any attacks much past midnight.

His luck ran out at 2:00 A.M. when listening devices or observers picked out the sound of his engines approaching Harwich, on England's east coast at least sixty-five miles northeast of his objective. Unfortunately, he was coming through at a relatively low altitude because he had good cloud cover and could make better speed. At least eight searchlights poked through the scattered clouds, enough to pinpoint his position. Almost immediately *L-13* received a bombardment of shells from pom-poms below. All of them missed except one. That was enough. Reported the navigator:

That devil flew right up from directly below. It came vertically through the keel and pierced a fuel line and two gas cells. There was no way we could make repairs and both bags emptied almost at once. But God was with us—*Gott mit uns*—and we did not burn.

Heinrich did not hesitate, despite his disappointment at failing to reach London. He ordered the bombardier to dump all bombs to lighten the ship, hoping we might be lucky enough to catch at least one of the bastards below who were shooting at us. Then we headed straight across forbidden terrain—a neutral zone—knowing that was the only way we could hope to reach friendly territory. We dumped almost 2,000 pounds of fuel, too, as the ship began to settle and we feared she would be uncontrollable. We barely made it, threatened by heavy rains and thunderheads. And even though we tossed overboard everything else that was loose or we could rip out, we landed much too solidly, cracking girders, smashing the control car, and bending the engine shafts badly.

I never saw Mathy quite so upset. He was usually as cool as ice. He kept blaming himself for flying over Harwich, which had such good ack-ack crews and a new detection system. But, you know, they had only recently been set up that way and our intelligence—not Heinrich—was at fault for not alerting us to the dangers.

For a time during the fall of 1915 Strasser's raids on London were threatened not by any improved enemy defense system but by political squabbles in Berlin. It all started because the general staff of the German army issued orders that army airships would be restricted in their attacks and could not go near the heart of London. This policy was tied in with military strategy and an old-line agreement that "open cities" which were largely civilian and had no military populations or wartime industries would not be subject to attack by warring armies. It was to Germany's advantage to avoid having to defend certain of its own cities, thus freeing more soldiers for duty in the trenches.

The navy, however, did not agree with this policy, largely because it was little involved with the cities in question. The chief of staff of the navy did concur, though, that he would not send airships over certain parts of London, especially "the northern quarter of the city inhabited chiefly by the poorer working classes." Another key part of this new strategy was that raids would be aimed at Liverpool on England's western coast, on the Irish Sea, because the port was receiving large shipments of supplies and munitions from the United States. Strasser was not happy about this decision, knowing that several hundred miles would be added to the round-trip distances his airships would be required to fly in order to get to that target instead of London or the east coast.

One raid of significance during this period of internal dissension occurred in mid-October, although it was considered a failure in terms of the mission's initial objective and ultimate achievements. This time five zeppelins were brought out of their sheds at Nordholz and Hage and sent aloft, again under the command of Heinrich Mathy. Four were forced to turn back before reaching the British capital, although two did some damage to docking and port facilities along the way. The only one to reach London was the *L-15* under the command of Commander Joachim Breithaupt, who was on his first mission to that city. Despite his neophyte status he made almost a perfect approach. He was challenged only once en route by anti-aircraft fire and even then got the better of the defenders when he dropped three explosive bombs and knocked out the gun position.

At 10:00 P.M. on 13 October 1915, he passed over the Houses of Parliament through a sky that was now cloudless and starlit. It all seemed like a scene from a romantic operetta rather than the life-and-death battle described by the press. A late-night debate was in session in the House of Commons when its toiling members heard the sound of antiaircraft fire and rushed outside to watch the unfolding drama.

"They were so tired of discussing taxes and legalities," explained one wag, "that they welcomed the choice of being blown up by a bomb rather than being bored to death."

A court reporter was so impressed by the vision he saw in the sky that he waxed poetic: "The giant airship was played upon by two searchlights and in their radiance she looked a thing of silvery beauty sailing serenely through the cool night, indifferent to the big gun roaring at her from the Green Park, whose shells seemed to burst in the manner of sparkling fireworks just below her, more like a welcome than a threat."

This esoteric sentiment was echoed by the fledgling commander Breithaupt, who later recorded his own thoughts at that instance. "The picture we saw was indescribably beautiful," he explained—"shrapnel bursting all around, our own bombs budding rosily, and the flashes from the antiaircraft batteries below . . . and over us the starlit sky!"

The enchantment of this spectacle was made more dramatic by an entirely new element on the broad mural of zeppelin warfare. As Breithaupt looked intently below, trying to zero in on his target even as he was overwhelmed by the impact of this unreal world, he spotted what looked like four huge moths bathing gloriously in the wash of the searchlights. They seemed as lovely and as unthreatening as white-robed ballerinas dancing across a floodlit stage. No one had told him about these participants in the midnight scene; in fact, no German had yet encountered them in any run over London. They were a new breed of flying thing: British monoplanes commandeered from the little makeshift aerodromes behind the front lines to strengthen the British defense network at home.

Although Breithaupt could see these flimsy little planes because of the exhaust flames from their engines, only one of the pilots detected the huge sky monster overhead. Perhaps their sight was too restricted by bulky helmets and oversize goggles or too blocked by the constant fanning of the pesky searchlights or too distracted by the whizzing flak that seemed to endanger them as much as it did the zeppelin. In any case, when the lone pilot bravely aimed the nose of his fragile craft skyward in what he must have then thought was a suicidal mission, the airship commander simply zoomed his ship skyward another fifteen hundred feet or so, knowing that it would take the monoplane almost half an hour to climb that far at that altitude.

As it happened, this little drama turned out to have been far more deadly than the Members of Parliament, the representative of the press, or the young commander could ever have imagined. By the time *L-15* had dropped its bomb load and headed back toward the dark skies and the Homeland beyond, 199 people lay dead or wounded on the bloody streets below. No bombs fell on the strategic targets—in this instance the Bank of England, the Admiralty, and the headquarters of the British navy. Instead, they decimated the crowded theatrical district, just missing the Gaiety Theatre, where the playbill was an American musical comedy entitled *Tonight's the Night*.

The audience of that production was fortunate indeed. The theatergoers inside heard the sound of artillery fire. But, instead of rushing out into the street, where some of them would surely have joined the victims, they remained inside because one of the actors turned to the audience as soon as he heard the noise and shouted with a broad grin: "Gun practice again!"

BRITISH RETALIATION

After returning from the mid-October strike against London Commander Joachim Breithaupt dispatched the required squadron report to headquarters. It was received and noted with special interest because of one entry that began "Over the city four aeroplanes were observed at 500 to 1,000 meters below our airship. They were clearly recognizable in the rays of the searchlights and by their exhaust flames." Although the young zeppelin skipper dismissed them as minor threats he had been able to evade much more easily than the bursts of shrapnel from the antiaircraft positions, Strasser was greatly concerned. Thus far, British aircraft had posed no problems for the Naval Air Division except for the flying-boat raids on airship bases, against which adequate defense measures had long since been taken.

Where did the planes come from? What types were they? How were they armed? Strasser activated his intelligence network and quickly discovered the basic facts. Five Royal Flying Corps planes in all had taken off from airfields to the east of London, identified as Sutton's Farm, Hainault Farm, and Joyce Green. One plane was forced to turn back with engine trouble and, as Breithaupt had accurately noted, of the four he saw below *L-15* only one seemed to have spotted the ship and tried to give chase. The attack had been futile because the planes in question were not armed with machine guns but simply with small incendiary bombs that had to be dropped by hand from above a targeted airship.

The German Naval Air Division called a halt to strikes against London for the rest of 1915, not because of concern about aeroplane defenses but simply because weather conditions over the North Sea were miserable and would continue to deteriorate with the onset of winter. Strasser used this slow period to broaden his training and recruitment programs, make improvements on his airships, and nag his superiors and the zeppelin works about deliveries of new ships that could be checked out and added to the growing fleet.

A few sorties, mainly over local waters, assisted naval units engaged in minesweeping, laying mines, and hunting British submarines, but these were inconsequential and largely squeezed into brief periods when the North Sea was not being whipped by gales. During this period Strasser suffered another devastating loss on the ground after a brand-new ship, the *L-18*, was delivered to the base at Tondern. While mechanics were filling one of her gas cells with hydrogen a spark touched off an explosion in a gasline. Although the accident at first seemed minor, taking place off to the side of the airship, a fuel tank exploded; this in turn spread flames to the nearest gas cell. Within seconds the double shed was racked by explosions and a fire that raged totally out of control for more than an hour.

This was the first of three fires in the Tondern shed, which seemed marked for disaster—the destruction on the ground of five zeppelins over the course of the next two years, all the result of accidents and in no way related to enemy action. Such setbacks would break the back of the most stout-hearted and dedicated commanders, and even Strasser felt near defeat each time one of these disasters occurred. He could face losses in raids over London, where it was understood by everyone involved that the risks were great and the odds were overwhelming, but it was disheartening to lose ships and men to these freak accidents on the ground.

No zeppelin raids on England were scheduled from mid–October until 31 January 1916, when a mass raid of nine airships was launched against the Midlands. The strike caused considerable damage to military and commercial facilities and left 183 Britons killed or injured. But most bombs missed their objectives, and this was the occasion on which *L-19* went down with the loss of all hands.

Another German loss came on 1 April, when Breithaupt again set out for a raid on London with the *L-15*, accompanied by the *L-13* under Mathy's command. They inflicted moderate damage and killed or wounded 112 people on the ground. However, *L-15* received a direct hit from AA that forced her to start losing altitude. Breithaupt attempted to make it back to friendly territory, but it was a losing battle. After jettisoning everything that could possibly be dumped overboard, he crash-landed in the

North Sea in a region known as Knock Deep. The British were quick to sight the wreckage and dispatched several gunboats to the scene. One of the crew members had drowned, but the others survived and were captured. Characteristically Breithaupt, the epitome of the handsome young Prussian officer, stood amid the floating wreckage in full uniform as the enemy arrived. It was said that he even wore one of his decorations, the Iron Cross, on the right breast of his tunic. At thirty-three, he knew this was the end of his military career. But, because of the growing hatred of the British who had suffered airship raids and realizing that the bombs he had recently dropped must have killed many civilians, he was certain he and his crew would be quickly tried by a military tribunal and executed.

"I take all the responsibility for the air raid upon myself," he said to the British officer in charge of the gunboats. "My men are not responsible and should not be punished."

A little more than a month later, another zeppelin met a similar fate when the *L-20*, under Kapitänleutnant Franz Stabbert, was struck by enemy shrapnel over England during a raid on 3 May. When the airship started losing altitude, Stabbert elected to try to reach neutral territory and managed to make a forced landing in Norway. He and nine other members of the crew were interned for the duration of the war and six were repatriated.

Such captures, however, were rare in World War I zeppelin warfare. For the most part, disabled craft either made it back to a home port or were lost with all aboard.

In the spring of 1916 the officers of the Naval Airship Division were greatly heartened by delivery of the *L-30*, which had been built at the Friedrichshafen factory. Scheduled for her initial flight on 23 May under command of Oberleutnant Buttlar, she was to be based at Nordholz and was the first of a new breed of superzeppelins. Radically improved over earlier models, *L-30* had a volume of two million cubic feet, almost twice that of previous types, weighed 80,000 pounds, and had a useful lift of 62,000 pounds. She was 650 feet long, taller than a ten-story building, and could attain a maximum speed of about sixty-five miles per hour, powered by six Maybach CX engines.

These new ships could reach a ceiling of thirteen thousand feet with a full combat load, higher than that after dumping bombs and climbing to get beyond antiaircraft range in an emergency. They were protected by ten machine guns from what the Germans expected would be future attacks by British planes equipped for high-altitude flight. Most important, the superzepps could carry five tons of high explosives and incendiaries and had much more sophisticated and accurate bombing instruments than their predecessors. In the early days of zeppelin warfare, bombs had literally been dropped by hand from the control gondola after the safety catch had been released so the explosive would be detonated on impact with the target. Later bombs were slung on racks under the gondola or belly of the airship so that they could be activated and released automatically. The accuracy still depended, however, on the seat-of-the-pants skill of the bombardier, who tried to relate the ground speed and altitude of the ship to such factors as wind, the size of the target, and the arc the missile would travel on its descent.

The new superzepps were equipped with bombsights that permitted the bombardier to make his calculations more quickly. They were positioned next to other instruments crucial to the accuracy of the operation such as the altimeter, wind gauge, and air-speed indicator. Yet a miscalculation in any single reading could seriously distort the overall reading. One of the most useful devices was the "test bomb" that was released during the approach to a target and made a trail of smoke to show the bombardier the arc and direction his live bombs would take when he was ready to fire.

The new *L-30* had one further distinction, though it would not be known for two more years: She was to undertake numerous missions, including attacks on London, but would be one of the few zeppelins to survive the war intact.

"The performance of the new breed of zeppelins has reinforced my conviction that England can be overcome by airships," reported Peter Strasser shortly after making test runs in *L-30* and her sister ship *L-31*, delivered six weeks later. "The airships offer a certain means of victoriously ending the war, inasmuch as the country will be deprived of the means of existence through increasingly extensive destruction of cities, factory complexes, railroads, dockyards, and harbor works with warships and merchant ships lying therein."

The Naval Air Division was back in its element when it scheduled its greatest raid of the year on 24 August, staging thirteen airships, including three of this new 30 class, against England. The British navy was alerted to the mass raid when radio silence was inadvertently broken and managed to direct fire from warships against six of the raiders. This deterrent, however, was mild by comparison with bad weather that had not been predicted by the unreliable meteorological stations of the period. Five ships were turned back by headwinds over the North Sea. Of the rest that managed to reach the British coast, all but one were frustrated by clouds and faulty navigation and dropped their loads on lesser targets than those intended. Only the brand-new *L-31* found its way through to London, where its major accomplishment was the destruction of a power station.

It was a poor showing, especially since this was the first airship to have done any significant damage to London in ten months.

During this period the Germans invented an ingenious, though highly controversial, accessory to the airship as a means of improving the accuracy of navigation, especially when there was heavy cloud cover. This was the "cloud car" that could be lowered by winch from the mother ship on a steel cable. Constructed of aluminum and shaped like a fat bomb in a horizontal position, it was characterized by four fins at the tail to stabilize it and a narrow cockpit to house an observer.

"There I hung, quite as though I had been in a bucket lowered into a well," said one occupant of this contraption as he described his experiences. "It was like having an upside-down periscope on a submarine. While the airship stayed hidden in the clouds as much as half a mile over my head, I could use my telephone to guide the navigator over the target.

"The first time out," he added ruefully, "I wondered whether any of the shower of bombs from above would land on my head instead of the ground."

The cloud car was controversial for two reasons: First, although it did hang below the clouds, there was no room for instruments and observers often could see very little that was helpful. Second, the cars had a negative drag effect on the zeppelin's progress and speed and (with cable and winch included) weighed almost half a ton, which otherwise might have added to the bomb load. The army favored the device generally and used it on numerous flights, but the navy considered it useless weight and operationally questionable.

Observers in the strange little car had experiences that ranged from the comic to the tragic. One was attacked by what he described as a hawklike bird who must have thought he was threatening its nest and swooped straight at him several times, barely clearing the narrow windscreen in front. Another observer was killed when the airship flew lower than expected and the car was dashed against a cliff.

Still another suffered a bizarre fate. When the airship was struck by flak and the crew had to jettison everything possible, he was told on the intercom that the winch had jammed because of enemy fire and the airship would cut its forward speed and come down low enough for the car to touch the ground. At that instant he was to notify the control car that he was on the ground and leap out because the cable would be instantly cut.

"You will be on your own," he was informed. "We are sorry but there is nothing else we can do except lighten the ship and try to get back to Germany."

This unique mission was accomplished, although the jolt when the car scraped the earth almost knocked its occupant out. He was able, however, to acknowledge that he was grounded. The cable was cut. The airship disappeared. And he found himself in a flat pasture, on British soil, and with no sense of location or direction.

For almost two months the stranded observer roamed enemy territory, hiding out in haylofts, cowsheds, and abandoned outbuildings by day and rummaging for food at night. Through road signs and once by venturing close to a village unseen, he judged eventually that he was somewhere in Sussex, not far from the English Channel. He was finally captured when a civilian coastal patrol spotted him crossing behind a farmhouse at dusk. He surrendered without a struggle, in fact relieved that he would no longer be on the run, and spent the rest of the war in a detention camp.

An event that occurred on 2 September 1916 drastically changed both the strategies and the effectiveness of German airships in the battle against Britain. On that date Peter Strasser scheduled a massive attack against London using a dozen of his zeppelins in conjunction with four ships dispatched by the German army. One of the latter group was the *SL-11*, under the command of Hauptmann Wilhelm Schramm—who had been born in London.

Technically, *SL-11* was not a zeppelin but a product of the

Schütte-Lanz factory, a direct competitor of the Zeppelin works founded by old Count Ferdinand von Zeppelin. In fact, calling an SL airship a zeppelin would be like referring to a Cadillac as a Ford.

The Luftfahrzeugbau Schütte-Lanz had been founded in 1909 in Württemburg, with government backing, by Johann Schütte and Karl Lanz, aeronautical engineers whose concepts of lighter-than-air craft differed substantially from those of the count and his engineering staff. The SLs, though Johnny-come-latelies, were rigid airships like their predecessors but soon began to surpass them in aerodynamic design. They were also superior in the matter of power-plant capabilities and control systems. The biggest disadvantage of the Schütte-Lanz construction was the use of lightweight wood instead of aluminum for the frame. Based in areas where the humidity was high and sent aloft through clouds and rain, the SLs tended to absorb moisture, which made them heavier and sometimes played havoc with joints that had been glued together.

It is doubtful that many of the British defense officers and men (or Germans outside the airship service, for that matter) could have recognized the difference between SLs and zeppelins or even knew that they were not one and the same. The *SL-11* had not yet developed any moisture problems. She had just been completed and had her maiden flight exactly one month before the 2 September raid. She was 570 feet long, almost 70 feet high, and was powered by four 140-horsepower Maybach engines that would produce a top airspeed of 60 miles per hour. She could carry a useful load of about 50,000 pounds, including two tons of bombs and incendiaries.

In general, the SLs and the zeppelins were much alike in the arrangement of separate hydrogen gas cells within the wire-braced framework and a system of gas tubes to collect escaping hydrogen and duct it safely into the atmosphere. Bomb compartments and water-ballast tanks were positioned along the keel inside the hull. Catwalks inside the lower hull permitted crew movement and vertical ladders gave access to machine-gun positions located on the top of the hull. Precarious though these were for the gunners, they had recently been installed as protection against expected attacks by British planes that were being equipped for night flights at high altitudes. Additional gun emplacements were located in the engine cars.

From the standpoint of numbers in service by the time of this raid, zeppelins outpaced SLs about six to one. The SL was also now becoming a poor second in the matter of altitude ceilings as the zeppelin engineers improved their ships in this respect to avoid enemy aircraft as well as antiaircraft guns. For this very reason—inability to climb rapidly out of range of enemy gunfire and attacks by fighter planes equipped to locate and shoot down airships—*SL-11* had a meeting with destiny on that fateful night in early September.

THE TURNING POINT

A continuing drizzle settled over the English countryside on 2 September 1916, a day to match the intense gloom of the British. Although the Germans were supposedly being pushed back at the front, the battles of the Somme and Verdun had been costly for the Allies. The British, with many unseasoned troops, had suffered most heavily.

At home the situation was one of general depression and frustration caused by many factors, not the least of which was that terrifying warning being heard more and more in the streets of London and several large industrial cities: "Zeppelins reported approaching!" It was now general knowledge that the Germans had perfected a new, higher-flying type of airship that could remain out of antiaircraft range while unleashing increasingly heavy loads of bombs and incendiaries on the populace below. Adding to the gloom was a recent report that the British army, which could ill afford to withhold fighting troops from the front lines, was having to commit more than fifty thousand men and millions of dollars worth of guns, planes, searchlights, and other costly equipment to the defense of England itself.

One of the least cheerful spots in all England that day was Sutton's Farm near London, where a long, flat strip of parched and oil-soaked pasture was occupied by B Flight, Thirty-Ninth Squadron of the Home Defense Wing. With the weather socked in, there had been nothing for the pilots and mechanics to do but sit around inside the makeshift frame-and-canvas hangar and grouse about the sad state of affairs. Even the usually shy and somewhat fragile-looking William Leefe Robinson, first lieutenant and flight commander, was sounding off relentlessly.

"Look at this bloody headline: What Is the Royal Flying Corps Doing?" He spat at a dog-eared newspaper clipping tacked to the operations bulletin board, fondling his small toothbrush mustache as he echoed the words. "What're we doing? Well, I can tell you we're sitting up here on our bloody arses listening to the grass grow!"

Robinson, twenty-one, a thin six-footer with piercing blue eyes, fair skin, and a round face, paced back and forth in the dreary hangar most of that afternoon. Occasionally, out of sheer boredom he hoisted his lanky frame up into the cockpit of one of the black-painted BE biplanes that had recently been equipped for night reconnaissance and armed with a new type of explosive bullet. At one time he patted one of the Lewis guns skeptically, shaking his head as though to indicate his belief that this really didn't seem like much of a zepp-killer.

It was depressing to look at this frail, inadequate equipment and accept the fact that all over England people—particularly the press—would be repeating the same timeworn question again: "What is the RFC doing?" Early fall surely meant a renewal of the zeppelin raids. Moreover, intelligence reports, which at that very moment lay on the adjutant's desk, made it clear that Peter Strasser, *Führer der Luftschiffe*, was including several of the new L-30-class airships on all forthcoming raids—the type that was said to climb higher, fly faster, carry larger bomb loads, and hit targets more accurately than any of the earlier types.

"Cheer up, Leefe," said Second Lieutenant Fred Sowrey as the afternoon waned. "One night we'll get a good crack at one of those flying gasbags, now that we're armed with something more deadly than bean-shooters."

"Don't bet any money on it," replied Robinson sourly. "Anyway, you're not likely to find out soon. It doesn't look like flying weather for tonight—even for Strasser and Company."

It would have astonished him to know that, even as he spoke, Fregatenkapitän★ Peter Strasser had already launched the greatest airship armada in history. Consisting of twelve navy zeppelins and four army airships, it was headed for its single objective: London.

Perhaps it was better that Robinson, Sowrey, and the other pilots of B Flight still had a few hours of blissful ignorance about the oncoming attack, in spite of their mind-numbing boredom. Had they known the zeppelins were over the North Sea, closing relentlessly, they might have spent the time in morbid contemplation of the RFC's apparent inability to cope with the German monsters. To date, despite sortie after sortie by RFC pilots during airship raids, no plane had yet downed or even disabled a zeppelin.

★ A World War I German naval aviation rank equivalent to rear admiral.

So-called incendiary bullets had been in use for at least a year and a half. As early as May 1915 a British flight sublieutenant named Reginald A. J. Warneford had used what were described as "flaming bullets" against an airship and reported that he had seen these, alternating with luminous tracer bullets, piercing the sides of the long cigar-shaped hull. Yet nothing had happened—no smoke, no fire, no rips in the envelope. The leviathan had moved relentlessly along its flight path as steadily as an elephant buzzed by a fly. Thereafter speculation was rampant that the Germans had perfected a form of insulation, an outer envelope of inert gas that prevented oxygen from mixing with the hydrogen within and thus keeping it nonflammable.

Would the same failure occur with the much-touted "new" type of incendiary bullet?

When the Royal Flying Corps initially tried to develop more high-powered incendiaries, some with explosives built in, the results had been disastrous. On several occasions the bullets had exploded prematurely in the machine-gun drums, seriously wounding pilots and gunners. It was also thought that this defect might have caused the loss of some twenty British planes that had crashed and burned while attempting to attack zeppelin raiders at night.

The situation had become so alarming and the British populace so bitter that, in early 1916, the Director of Air Organization had ordered a full-scale effort to try to perfect some completely new type of incendiary that would be effective yet safe. By April his "progress" had been limited to an official memorandum, copies of which could be found tattered and scrawled with less-than-flattering remarks in many an RFC billet:

It is proposed to issue shortly an explosive bullet for use against Zeppelins, and in this connection I am directed to inform you that its use is strictly restricted to firing from an airplane against an airship.

The battle of words was on, but it was also accompanied shortly by some results. One incendiary was known as the Buckingham .303; others were the Pomeroy and the Brock. All three had been used dramatically to demonstrate how they could set fire to gas-filled balloons at several hundred yards. Yet all through the summer months the zeppelins had continued their raids and had been shot at repeatedly by British planes equipped with one or other of these new incendiaries—without effect.

Almost frantically during this period the British air ministry continued its race to perfect incendiaries that would be effective as well as to redesign planes and engines that could climb higher and faster to try to match the ever-improving performances of the airships. It was a losing battle because every time the British moved a step forward the Germans had already moved a similar step.

Earlier that dismal, rainy September second, actions that were under way in Germany were directly to affect Lieutenant William Leefe Robinson and the other pilots of B Flight—and, in fact, the entire Royal Flying Corps. All over Germany, at the great zeppelin sheds at Nordholz and Ahlhorn and other airship bases, the early afternoon echoed with the sound of powerful Maybach engines roaring into life and the barked orders of Luftschiffe officers as they eased their behemoths out of the hangars and lifted slowly into the sullen skies.

The sixteen zeppelins and Schütte-Lanzes that began around 2:00 P.M. to rendezvous over the North Sea, their slick noses pointed westward toward England, represented the largest airship armada ever assembled for an attack. Between them they carried almost fifty tons of bombs, ranging from small incendiaries and 25-pounders to 650-pounders—which would later become popularly known as blockbusters because of their devastating capacity for destruction. The best of the ships, represented by two in the new L-30 class, could climb to altitudes of more than fifteen thousand feet, well beyond the known ceiling of the latest British fighter planes. Their climb rate and altitude range were limited less by technology than by the ability of humans to function at those heights.

Some of these ships were from 600 to 650 feet long and all carried enough fuel to operate from four to six engines for twenty-four hours, plenty of time for a round trip to London or the Midlands, even with headwinds and delays. All were equipped with machine guns, both topside and near the engine bays, to ward off fighters.

The September raid was planned as a way of proving to the British that England could be brought to her knees by the mounting fury of zeppelin warfare. In his dedicated, purposeful manner Strasser had announced that this time every effort would be made to see that all sixteen ships reached London in such a manner as to pound the city relentlessly by a succession of attacks. Privately he admitted that a prime target would be the British Admiralty itself: "I expect to lay some impressive eggs right in its doorway."

He was convinced that he could shatter the enemy's morale if he could get in a strong blow at Naval Intelligence headquarters and the Royal Command. To ensure success, Strasser announced that he was assigning his most experienced officers to the individual commands—including Buttlar, Mathy, and Ernst Lehmann. As for himself, he would go along as an observer in the newest ship, *L-32*, under the command of the able Werner Peterson.

Thus the massive raid began.

★　★　★

Late that afternoon, as Robinson and Sowrey began feeling pangs of hunger and wondering what the mess officer had dreamed up for supper at the Sutton's Farm field, events of a more disturbing nature were taking place elsewhere in England. At the radio monitoring station at Hunstanton on The Wash, the great bay halfway up the east coast on the North Sea, operators were recording fragments of messages in German code—a much greater volume than normal.

As the pieces were put together and partially decoded by Air Intelligence specialists, the pattern became apparent. As many as a dozen—possibly more—German ships had left their bases and were proceeding somewhere. The silence that followed each brief message gave no clue as to what was in the wind. It could be a series of training flights. Or a dispersal of airships to act as observers for a unit of the imperial fleet, a common operation.

Or it could be a mass raid against England.

By as early as five-thirty that afternoon it was evident to British Naval Intelligence that these airships not only had cleared their hangars but were well out over the North Sea. By this time the weather had lifted in a manner more favorable to raiders than to defenders. On one hand, it was now clear enough for accurate navigation; on the other, it was overcast enough for airships to take full advantage of cloud cover while maneuvering into position over intended targets.

Intelligence notified the Home Guard to be on the lookout for raiders—visually by observers along the coast and acoustically through huge audiophonic devices nicknamed "mechanical ears" that could pick up the distant hum and beat of gasoline engines long before human ears could do so.

"I don't get it. I just don't get it at all." Commander Ellery Smith, an interpreter for British Naval Intelligence and a former longtime resident of Germany, had spread the brief wireless messages out before him and had partially identified the airships whose messages had been intercepted. "We have here at least a dozen naval zeppelins. But we also have some Schütte-Lanz ships belonging to the Army. The Army and the Navy—they don't mix. Just don't mix. Not those chaps." He paused. "Not unless, of course, we have in the making the biggest bloody combined operation ever mounted by the Boche."

Intelligence continued the decoding process, noting another factor, too, received from meteorological stations: The wind was about ten knots from the west, a favorable set-up for a raid involving slight headwinds for the trip to the target but resulting in a steady, helpful push for the return flight to base.

At nine-fifteen that night headquarters of the Home Defense transmitted warnings to all posts along the coast and in the heartland around London: "Air Raid Alert!"

Not until almost ten o'clock did Lieutenant Robinson receive the air-raid-alert warning. By that time the keeper of the Haisboro lightship, ten miles off the Norfolk coast, was talking excitedly over the undersea telephone cable leading from his vessel to a defense command post ashore.

"We've got about half a dozen gasbags over our heads somewhere," he sputtered. "We've spotted two of the buggers and our orthophone has picked up the sound of more damned Maybachs than I've ever heard in my life. I tell you, something big is happening!"

Within a few more minutes the keeper had reported the engine sounds diminishing and gave an estimated heading. Then Intelligence began receiving reports all up and down the coast from listening posts, lookouts, and wireless stations. By ten-thirty the first bombs were reported falling on English soil. The raid had begun.

After receiving the initial attack warning, Lieutenant Robinson checked out his black BE2c with *2092* painted on its nose. This wide-wing biplane was known as the workhorse of Britain's Royal Flying Corps and was used more for reconnaissance than combat. It had two cockpits and carried a single Lewis machine gun that could be positioned on either of two mountings. Most BE2 models were equipped with four-blade propellers that allowed them to climb to high altitudes, where the air was thin. Since Robinson and his fellow pilots usually went aloft alone rather than with a gunner or observer, they had an extra advantage when it came to climbing higher and faster.

After Robinson was sure his plane was ready for action, he sprawled out on a hard army cot to await further orders. If things went the way they usually did, he thought to himself, he would still be on the cot by dawn and nothing would have happened. The chances were that the zepps were heading to Norfolk or The Wash, hitting at the coast and the Midlands rather than London, some twenty miles to the southwest of the Sutton's Farm airfield.

Just after eleven o'clock the phone near his cot jingled. Robinson, who had half dozed off, picked it up sleepily.

"Take immediate air-raid action!" came the crisp order.

Robinson leaped up. He had not had a chance to tangle with an enemy airship since the previous May, and that encounter had been extremely frustrating. After an hour's chase through a moonless sky, he had come close enough to a zeppelin to run off three full drums of incendiaries in the direction of the huge dark shape with no more result than if he had been a sunfish trying to bite a whale.

Well, at least there was some excitement. Chasing gasbags at night was not exactly the safest sport in the world. He still remembered with horror how two of his fellow pilots in Squadron 39 had paid the price for trying to help maintain England's Home Defense. Only a few months earlier they had crashed while trying to feel their way down to the strip in the uncertain light of a row of burning buckets of gasoline. One pilot had survived, partially blinded. The other had emerged from the fiery wreckage of his plane as a human torch, screaming in agony as he ran fifty yards across the oily grass before anyone could get to him and douse him with water. He lingered in the hospital for three days and nights in excruciating pain before dying.

Then, too, not a few of his friends and colleagues had received painful, sometimes serious, burns and wounds about the face and head when incendiaries and explosive bullets had gone off prematurely before leaving the Lewis guns. These sacrifices might have been worth it, Robinson often thought, if only the RFC had something to show for all the time, money, and casualties involved in futile zepp-hunting. But, to date, the score was an absolute goose egg.

By 11:11 P.M. *2092* had been pushed into position for takeoff. The rain had stopped. There were scattered clouds on the dark horizon, but no sign of the enemy and no sound of distant Maybachs humming across the sky.

"I told you we'd get another crack at the Huns." Second Lieutenant Fred Sowrey ran breathlessly out to help Robinson get his prop started since the routine flight attack plan did not call for him to take to the air until fifteen minutes after his flight commander was airborne.

"Maybe. The only crack we're likely to get though is when we try to set down again on this bloody little cow pasture," retorted Robinson. "I don't like the way this ground fog builds up."

As the mechanics finished lighting the flare pots for takeoff the pilots could clearly see that a thick blanket of mist was creeping across the field from a distant grove of low-lying trees. Deceptively soft-looking, it had been the cause of a score of accidents and at least two casualties as pilots attempted to come home in the dark, dangerously low on fuel. The mist, he knew, would thicken as the night wore on.

For a few moments the night was strangely silent. At exactly 11:30 Robinson could hear the bong of a steeple clock somewhere to the southeast, probably near the outskirts of London. Then the silence was shattered by the sounds of swearing as his mechanic fumbled for the wooden propeller.

"Petrol on!" barked Robinson mechanically. "Choke out. Contact!"

After each command the mechanic answered like an echo, then swung the heavy prop. This was followed by more swearing until, after several tries, the cold engine caught and the flimsy craft began shaking and quivering like a branch of dry leaves in the wind.

Robinson checked out the dashboard light, an innovation for night fighters though there was not much in the way of instruments to light up. He patted the breech of the Lewis gun for good luck. He had already inspected every inch of it a dozen times that afternoon as well as meticulously examining the ammunition drums to make sure there was not the slightest bit of grit or grease that could cause jamming or misfiring. The drums had been loaded alternately with the new Pomeroy and Brock incendiaries, named after the ordnance officers who had invented them.

"If one kind doesn't blow up in your face the other will!" was the cynical comment one of his fellow officers had made when the official RFC memorandum had been distributed to orient squadrons on the loading of their machine guns.

"Chocks away!" The mechanic yanked the restraining blocks away from the thin wire wheels. This was it. Robinson gave his ship full throttle, felt the wheels bump protestingly along the rutted grass, and was quickly airborne.

For the better part of an hour he climbed, following a predetermined flight pattern destined to bring his plane to the general cruising altitude used by airships. That way, as soon as a pilot spotted one, he would presumably be at about the same height rather than having to waste time climbing farther. He knew that other pilots from Squadron 39, unseen, were also in the air around him, each covering a designated sector of the dark sky. With the kind of scattered clouds that prevailed that night there was little chance that any zeppelin could sneak through the protective network of aircraft around London without being spotted. Yet Robinson saw nothing. He cut his engine (a risky maneuver since sometimes a lot of altitude could be lost before getting it turning over again) to listen for the sound of Maybachs. Nothing.

The darkness was velvety and complete. Even the great city of London, usually a sparkle of light, was black. It had taken the British a long time to admit that they had to submit to blackouts. But by this period in the war, after several disastrous raids that hit well-lighted targets, they had set up a procedure for extinguishing all city lights as soon as air-raid warnings were received.

At 12:40 A.M. Robinson saw the darkness split by searchlights north and east of his position. At one moment he thought he heard the distant sound of bombs exploding, but he could not be sure because of the engine's roar and the vibration caused by the bitterly cold wind. He switched on the dashboard light for no more than three seconds and noted that his altimeter registered 11,000 feet. He pushed the BE2c still higher at about three-quarters throttle, saving a margin of power for a final climb to the plane's ceiling if necessary—about 13,000 feet.

Even with his flying suit, leather helmet, and heavy gloves he could feel the chill September air as the wind whistled through the cramped open cockpit. Slowly the altimeter needle climbed to 12,000, then 12,300. The cold steadily increased.

At 1:08 A.M. he sighted the first enemy ship.

It was the army *LZ-98*, under the command of Ernst Lehmann, the reserve officer who would later work closely with Hugo Eckener in the development of dirigibles and peacetime airship travel. Lehmann was a congenial man who was well liked by fellow officers and other ranks alike. A natural-born leader rather than a technician like Eckener, he seemed always to be as cool and self-controlled under fire as when he was in nothing more exciting than a training mission. Enlisted men and younger officers were thankful when they were assigned to a mission under his command.

The *LZ-98* was proceeding over the Thames near Gravesend and had come under heavy fire from ground batteries at Dartford and Tilbury. When Robinson spotted her, she was in the final process of dumping her bomb load over an area that seemed to have no military significance. As it turned out, Lehmann had intended to bomb docks along the Thames but was far off course. The failure to sight the right target may have been caused in part by the arrival of Robinson, who diverted the enemy when he pushed his plane at full throttle to the attack. With that the airship climbed to an altitude of nearly fourteen thousand feet and headed to the northeast in partial cloud cover at sixty miles an hour.

Disgusted, Robinson gave up the futile chase. He did not realize then how fortunate he was to have pushed his little plane so high. He saw what he thought was a searchlight beam, but there was something peculiar about it. The white swath was horizontal, not vertical, and all at once he realized what this was: a searchlight sweeping the length of an elongated shape. A cloud? No, it was another airship. Robinson banked his plane sharply to head in that direction, noting at the same time that bursts of artillery fire were exploding quite far beneath the airship, evidence that she was at a considerable altitude.

This was the *SL-11*, under the command of Hauptmann Wilhelm Schramm; she had headed in from the North Sea over the river Crouch and reached the London area shortly after 1:00 A.M. Schramm had dropped bombs on a number of northern suburbs before being picked up by the searchlight Robinson had sighted.

Robinson was now at 12,900 feet, an ideal height since the airship appeared to be about five hundred feet lower, a fine position for a diving attack once he moved within firing range. As the distance narrowed, the RFC pilot was filled with a sudden surge of awe that he, in this flimsy little craft put together with metal, fabric, wire, and wood, should be charging against a monster six hundred feet long and more than eighty feet high. The only thing he had in his favor at the moment was the sure knowledge that he had not yet been spotted despite the flames from his exhaust. He did not then know it, but two other pilots from Squadron 39 had also sighted this airship and were trying to get within range.

Then, all at once, the great shape disappeared—completely, absolutely, as though whisked away by magic. The ship's commander must have purposely headed into a protective cloud bank to evade the searchlights and antiaircraft fire from the ground. "Of all the rotten luck!" Robinson shouted into the wind in disgust, but his voice was so caught up by the slipstream of air and carried away that he felt as though no sound had emerged from his tightly scarfed throat.

He circled the area for perhaps ten minutes. Then, according to RFC standing orders, he resumed a zigzag search-and-look flight pattern. It was 1:40 A.M. now, almost time for him to return to base and hope that the ridiculously small patch of landing strip at Sutton's Farm would not be completely blanketed by mist. There were alternative fields and each pilot was given carte blanche in the event of engine trouble, low fuel, or damage from enemy fire. But the other fields would be just as likely to be layered in mist—perhaps even more so. He wondered whether Fred Sowrey was anywhere in the vicinity and whether he too might have made an airship sighting.

At 1:52 A.M. he was almost resigned to pointing the nose down and heading for home when he noticed a reddish glow northeast of London and in the general direction of his own base. It could mean only one thing: Enemy bombs had found a mark and started fires. And where there were bombs there would be an airship. He opened his throttle wide and headed straight for the fiery glow, maintaining his altitude of almost thirteen thousand feet.

Searchlights flicked the sky again, playing off clouds and the smoke blossoms formed by the ack-ack bursts. As he skirted a towering bank of clouds he spotted his target again, her nose just pushing out of the cloud cover, possibly so the bombardier could get a quick look below and drop the rest of his bomb load. This time, Robinson decided not to be diverted by his advantage in altitude and a more careful evaluation of his position. Instead, he immediately pushed the joy stick slightly forward and headed directly for the gas bag. He realized that he would have only a couple of passes at most before the crew, realizing they were under attack, could sneak the ship back into the cloud cover. Then he would have to call it quits because he was very low on petrol.

All at once, Robinson was half blinded by an explosion that seemed to be right under him. He threw his hands up in front of his face instinctively, certain that one of the machinegunners atop the zepp or in the engine pods had sighted the plane and fired a burst of explosive shells in his direction. The BE-2 rocked crazily, almost flipping out of control. Then he realized what had happened. He was smack in the middle of a barrage of antiaircraft fire from the British defense positions below. Naturally, in the darkness and with the confusion of ever-changing searchlight patterns, gunnery officers could not detect the tiny black speck in the sky that represented one of their own fighter planes.

Robinson had two choices: He could set off Very* signals from a handgun supplied for the purpose, to request that ground batteries hold their fire, or he could ignore the danger and continue on course. Preferring not to reveal his presence and position to the Germans and attract fire that would be just as deadly, or more so, he left his Very pistol in its rack. Now the plane was wobbling and bobbing in the sky like a novice rider atop a spirited horse. But the airship was almost within range.

There she was, that immense nose coming right at him with all the deadliness of a giant shark bearing down on a hapless swimmer. He estimated the distance as fifteen hundred yards . . . twelve hundred yards . . . a thousand yards. Still the airship's crew seemed oblivious to his presence, perhaps because all eyes were turned to the ground and the final targets. More bombs were falling now through the scattered cloud formation into which the airship had moved from its protective cloud bank. The dull glow from below suddenly blossomed as a bomb found a flammable target. This was just what Robinson might have hoped for, since it illuminated the airship's envelope more clearly.

He was five hundred yards away now and about two hundred yards below the airship, charging at full throttle. He had more than enough speed as he passed along the underside of the tre-

---

* A Very pistol was a specialized kind of handgun invented by an American engineer, E. W. Very, shortly before World War I. It was loaded with a large cartridge which, when triggered, would shoot colored flares in whatever direction the barrel was pointed. It was used for signalling, not as a weapon. However, there were cases when it was used for ignition when a downed pilot, for example, wanted to set his fighter plane on fire to avoid its capture by the enemy.

mendous black shape to zoom upward and rake the airship's underbelly with an entire drum of Brock and Pomeroy incendiaries. He was so close that he could distinguish the silhouettes of officers and men in the control car and the engine ports. He watched the tracer bullets (which were phosphorescent and helped him aim the Lewis gun) bite into the airship's fabric.

Nothing happened.

Now he was past the tail of the ship and banking sharply around for a second run. This was the moment when long hours of dull, monotonous training and practice would come into critical focus. They made it possible for him to control the plane with his feet and one elbow while he reloaded the Lewis gun with a second drum.

There was no doubt now that his presence was known. The *SL-11* veered sharply to port to make for the nearest cloud cover. Within seconds she would complete another disappearing act. At the same time the sky seemed to echo with the sharp crack-crack of explosive fire from at least six of the machine-gun positions aboard.

The plane's sharp turn not only threw their aim out of true but gave Robinson the few moments he needed to catch up to his prey again and rake the lower belly of the port side. He was within a hundred yards now of the airship's own altitude. He watched his second drum of incendiaries, mixed with tracers, pour into the wall of fabric.

Still nothing happened.

Robinson swore in a mighty bellow of frustration and rage: "Those goddamned duds! I might as well be tossing popcorn at the Huns!" The image of the newspaper headline flashed across his conscience: What Is the Royal Flying Corps Doing? What indeed! He'd ask those bloody bastards with the ordnance department what *they* were doing. And what were those bloody civilians doing who worked in the munitions factories, filling the bullet shells with talcum powder?

Automatically he wheeled his plane around again, doing his juggling act as he steered with his feet and began reloading another drum. He doubted that he could get in a third pass before his target vanished. But he'd try.

Robinson's altimeter read 11,800 as he came in the third time, almost on a level with *SL-11*, which had nosed down somewhat to seek the cloud cover. His course had brought him around so that his approach was toward the starboard aft end of the airship. Coming up astern would give him more time to aim carefully— perhaps he had been hitting the keel section and not the inner gasbags themselves. Even so, it was a dangerous position because he was in a direct line of fire from one of the engine gunners. The antiaircraft fire was also intense, although so far no shrapnel had seemed to hit either the airship or his own plane.

When he was two hundred yards behind and slightly below the giant tail fins, Robinson aimed carefully once more at the belly of *SL-11* and steadily squeezed the trigger of the Lewis gun, this time focusing his fire more on one location than raking the airship. Perhaps a concentration of bullets would be more effective than a skip-and-jump strategy. Again he could see the stream of tracers, alternating with the Pomeroy and Brock incendiaries, biting into one particular section of the fabric. The gun chattered angrily, then stopped as it jammed and he struggled in vain to clear it.

Of all the goddamned luck!

Robinson was about to repeat his tirade of oaths to the gods and the clouds when he suddenly became transfixed by a chilling sight. Just forward of the tail section, where the incendiaries had penetrated the fabric, a rosy glow appeared, as though a crew member had switched on a huge lamp within the translucent envelope.

Within a few seconds the entire stern had erupted into a tremendous explosion of flame. The young British pilot felt a sharp, angry blast of intense heat against his face even behind the protective goggles and scarf. The BE2c rocked crazily out of control and threatened to fall into a tailspin. For a few more seconds Robinson remained motionless, hypnotized by the awesome sight and momentarily unable to move or think or act.

Suddenly he realized to his horror that the course of his uncontrolled plane and the slowing down of the *SL-11* would carry him directly under the huge hull, now blazing from bow to stern. Desperately he wrestled with the controls to get his plane back on an even keel. Just as the burning airship seemed ready to settle down on top of him and envelop plane and pilot in her fiery embrace, Robinson managed to sideslip away from certain death.

But death was all around him. He could see the figures of officers and men diving from the burning ship, preferring to be dashed to the ground than to be grilled alive in the crumpling framework. He had heard that German airships carried no parachutes, their commanders preferring to sacrifice them in return for carrying slightly larger bomb loads. It was obviously true, for he saw not a single chute opening up. And anyway, he decided grimly, who could have used a parachute with this fiery behemoth falling on top of him?

As soon as he was safely away from the holocaust, Robinson excitedly dropped a parachute flare and fired off a few rounds of Very lights. He wanted his compatriots on the ground to realize that a plane was up there in the sky and had been responsible for the successful attack. Then it was all over. The twisted framework plunged earthward through a cloud layer, leaving an overwhelming odor of burning oil and scorched fabric, and the pilot was alone in the cold, dark night. With a numbed sensation he pointed the nose of his plane toward the warmer layers of air below him and dived jubilantly toward the earth. Leveling off at two thousand feet, he could sight enough silhouettes of landscape features and structures to head for Sutton's Farm, which he realized all at once would be a touch-and-go affair, what with his petrol running out. Behind him the doomed airship was still settling in a huge pillar of flame, the fire so bright that it illuminated buildings all along the northeastern perimeter of London.

As he had expected, the ground was heavily blanketed by mist, so much so that the flare pots along the airstrip were barely visible at less than a thousand feet. Yet Robinson, emotionally overcome by what he had seen and done, could not even recall later just how he had brought his plane in for a landing or whether he had experienced any difficulty. He only knew that he was all at once back on the ground and being welcomed by several mechanics and fellow pilots who had seen the huge glare in the sky from afar and wondered what had happened.

The time was 2:43 A.M.

Within fifteen minutes Robinson was flat on his bunk, sound asleep.

(TOP) Count Ferdinand von Zeppelin in the control car of one of his earliest zeppelins at Friedrichshafen.
(BOTTOM) The count and his wife during a reception honoring him for his achievements in the design and production of airships (Credit: National Air and Space Museum, Smithsonian Institute).

Peter Strasser, who pioneered the development of zeppelins as an attack force, headed up the German Naval Airship Division. His death in action aboard one of the newest ships, *L-70*, on 5 August 1918, marked the end of Zeppelin warfare (Credit: *Bundesarchiv*, Koblenz).

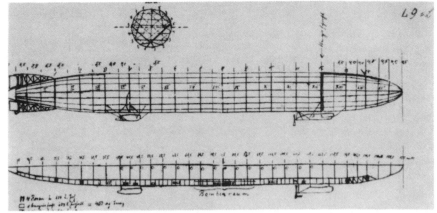

A rough sketch of the *L-9* prior to the engineering designs, showing how this airship would be longer than contemporary ships in service and capable of carrying a larger bomb load. Note the emphasis in the lower center on *Bombenraum*, calculated to house bombs and provide more accurate sighting and release mechanisms than in the past (Credit: *Bundesarchiv*, Koblenz).

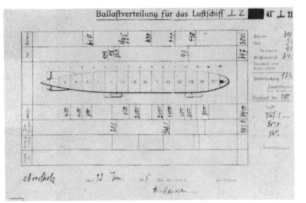

A ballast sheet for the German airship *L-11*. These forms, printed on loose-leaf pads before each flight, recorded the amount of water ballast, fuel, bombs, equipment, and personnel to be carried and how they were to be distributed in the various sections. This form was completed at the Nordholz base for a flight on 12 June 1915, which apparently was a trial run and not a bombing raid (Credit: *Bundesarchiv*, Koblenz).

This pattern of searchlights, catching a marauding airship in the night sky over London, graphically shows how determined the British were to suppress zeppelin raids on their cities (Credit: National Air and Space Museum, Smithsonian Institute).

Separate steering wheels for rudders and elevators are shown inside the control car of the German airship *SL-15*. The engine-control levers at the lower right, as well as other controls, were copied from those on board naval ships and were not always as effective as they needed to be when aloft (Courtesy of the late Captain Hans von Schiller).

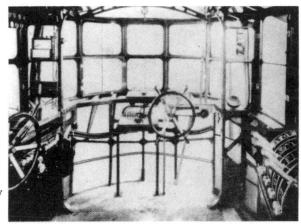

Early zeppelins were equipped with makeshift machine gun positions atop their hulls after British fighter planes were modified for high-altitude operations. This sketch by German artist Felix Schormstadt depicts a gunner and observer in action while a trio of British biplanes circles for an attack (Courtesy of the late Captain Hans von Schiller).

A German airship, *L-20* (formerly *LZ-59*), which crash-landed on the coast of Norway on 3 May 1916 after a raid on England. Ten survivors of its crew were interned and six were repatriated by Norway (Credit: National Air and Space Museum, Smithsonian Institute).

L-30, one of the most successful zeppelins, was commissioned 30 May 1916 and made numerous raids on England until it was taken out of service at the end of 1917. The airship was later broken up and its parts were delivered to the Allies in Belgium (Credit: National Air and Space Museum, Smithsonian Institute).

This "sub–cloud" car, made of duralumin, was suspended from the airship by a thin steel cable and lowered to the desired height by a winch. Thus the zeppelin could remain in the clouds, hidden from antiaircraft units on the ground, while the observer in the car used a telephone to direct the dropping of the bombs. The tail fins kept the car steady while the airship was in motion (Credit: National Air and Space Museum, Smithsonian Institute).

Lieutenant William Leefe Robinson of Britain's Royal Flying Corps (RFC) became the first pilot to shoot down a zeppelin. On the night of 2 September 1916, he went aloft in his fragile *BE2c* fighter plane to intercept airships coming in for a raid over London. At an altitude of some thirteen thousand feet, after climbing for an hour, he attacked the *SL-11* with incendiary bullets from his Lewis gun and brought it down in flames (Credit: National Air and Space Museum, Smithsonian Institute).

While mechanics work over a disabled Maybach engine in the rear gondola of *LZ-38*, a machine gunner peers anxiously for enemy aircraft. The original sketch, in color, was rendered by Felix Schormstadt, a German artist who was commissioned to illustrate bombing flights based entirely on his observation of airships on the ground and recollections of the officers and men who saw action (Courtesy of the late Captain Hans von Schiller).

This wreckage (unidentified) of a zeppelin that had been shot down in flames over England provides a clear picture of the aluminum skeleton of a typical rigid airship. The nearby house provides a reference for the enormous size of these ships (Credit: National Air and Space Museum, Smithsonian Institute).

The British, with little experience in designing or constructing airships prior to World War I, used lighter-than-air craft largely for observation purpose or home defense. This official government painting depicts blimps of the Royal Navy escorting a convoy off the coast in waters frequented by German submarines (Credit: British Imperial War Museum).

This artist's rendering from World War I shows a conventional airship control gondola, circa 1917, in comparison with the crude car designed for one of Count Zeppelin's early ships (Credit: National Air and Space Museum, Smithsonian Institute).

Inside the control gondola of a zeppelin of an advanced type in late 1917. The enlisted man at the right is the radio operator. In the background the commander and his executive officer operate the elevator and rudder wheels to keep the ship on course (Credit: National Air and Space Museum, Smithsonian Institute).

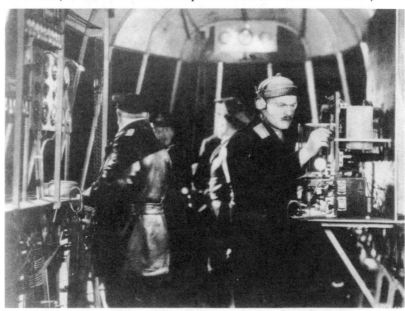

A zeppelin (unknown, but probably of the 30 class) on maneuvers with the German fleet in 1917. Although these huge airships could serve well as observers, they were useless in making attacks on enemy fleets and could easily have been supplanted by blimps or other small lighter-than-air craft (Credit: National Air and Space Museum, Smithsonian Institute).

L-48 photographed from below on its maiden flight on 22 May 1917. The Germans expected great success with this new class, but *L-48* was shot down in flames less than a month later at Theberton while in a raid over Suffolk, England. Miraculously two of her officers survived the crash (Credit: National Air and Space Museum, Smithsonian Institute).

As part of the defense against aerial attacks, the British experimented with the installation of platforms on naval vessels from which fighter planes could take off to intercept zeppelins before they reached the English coast. This scene shows what appears to be a modified version of the Sopwith Camel taking off from such a platform (Credit: National Air and Space Museum, Smithsonian Institute).

L-45 after making a forced landing at Sisteron, France, on 20 October 1917. Its surviving officers and enlisted men, seventeen in all, were taken prisoner by the French who later dismantled the airship (Courtesy of the late Captain Hans von Schiller).

By the time it was built in 1929, the British airship *R-101* was the biggest and most expensive flying machine the world had ever seen. It was 131 feet in diameter and 777 feet in length—more than three times the length of a Boeing 747 (Credit: British Imperial War Museum).

A seared and twisted skeleton was all that remained of the *R-101* after it crashed and exploded near Beavais, France on 5 October 1930. Described as "safe as a house" by one of its notable passengers, Lord Thomson of Cardington, on that fateful journey, the airship proved to be Thomson's funeral bier, along with that of forty-seven other victims (Credit: British Imperial War Museum).

AFTERMATH

The impact of Lieutenant William Leefe Robinson's accomplishment was such that all London went mad. For hours after the downfall of *SL-11*, people sang and danced in the streets. Sirens that had previously been sounded only to announce air raids let loose as their operators discarded all caution and openly flaunted regulations. Locomotive whistles squealed in the cool night air; auto Klaxons along the city streets were earsplitting; ships' foghorns along the docks blared ceaselessly; church bells rang; all sizes and types of noisemakers in the possession of jubilant citizens were operated to the fullest.

In the dark skies above England the effect of this historic event was completely different. The nearest ship to *SL-11* was *L-16* (under Kapitänleutnant Erich Sommerfeldt), which had dropped part of her bomb load on Norwich and was cruising less than a mile to the north of the ill-fated ship when, as one of her machine gunners in a post at the top of the hull said later, "The sky lit up bright as day. At first I thought that our own ship had been struck and was exploding beneath me. Then I saw that it was one of our sister ships on the raid."

The officers and men of *L-16* believed the explosion had been caused by an artillery shell—until the navigator trained his telescope on the falling ship and let out a quick exclamation of disbelief: "My God! There's a plane over there. It just finished attacking. We've got to get the hell out of here before we're next in line!"

Sommerfeldt took instant evasive action and headed at full speed on a northeasterly course for the coast. Behind them they spotted what looked like the silhouette of a fighter plane against the glare in the sky, but they had no intention of sticking around to find out.

The brand-new *L-32* was near Luton, about twenty-two miles northwest of London. She had been badly delayed by early snow squalls and had iced up and become so tailheavy that Peterson ordered the release of several 110-pound bombs to make her more manageable. He might have solved the problem by flying at a lower altitude, but they were too close to the ring of artillery posts around the capital and he needed every foot of height he could get to reduce their danger of being struck. When he clearly saw the *S-11* going down in flames, he could not control his emotions and wept openly in the control car. His august passenger and observer, Peter Strasser, controlled his feelings but was even more undone than his subordinate at the sight. What he did not know yet and would discover later with great shock was that the ship had been knocked out of the air by a small plane, not by an artillery barrage.

The moment he feared had become a reality. The British were perfecting fighter planes capable of matching zeppelins in both altitude and rate of climb and, furthermore, had the ordnance and ammunition necessary to shoot them down.

On board the *LZ-98*, which two hours earlier had evaded Robinson's attack by climbing rapidly and seeking cloud cover, Ernst Lehmann heard his first officer let out a sudden piercing shriek. When he turned to find out what was wrong with the man, he saw *SL-11* enveloped in flames, a horrendous vision of the fate he himself had narrowly missed. For other airship commanders, some of whom could see the fire in the sky from as far as fifty miles away, this disaster was the handwriting on the wall. It was reported that "six of the remaining German commanders abandoned the attack and ran for home, shaken by the disaster they had witnessed and depressed by its dreadful portent."

Even had no ship been destroyed on the raid they would have had reason to be shaken. Of some 463 bombs carried in the raid on England, only a handful actually hit targets in the London area, and with relatively minor damage. They knew, too, that Strasser—formerly so optimistic about the ability of zeppelins to break England's back—had been plunged into a deep depression after the raid. For days he was seldom seen, and then only going to and from conferences with his close friend and most reliable technical adviser, Ernst Lehmann.

Adding salt to their wounds, the German army made it known confidentially that it was risking no more of its men, officers, or equipment in raids on British cities. It would confine its activities to such operations as troop support, supply, and aerial observation.

As intelligence reports sifted into official German circles from England, the gloom deepened because of the great uplift the failed raid had had on the British morale. The *SL-11*, whose scorched skeleton fell to the north of London in a field behind a pub, became a kind of grim monument to England's glory and determination. The little village of Cuffley, where the ship came down, became the site of a virtual pilgrimage as people came from dozens of surrounding locales on foot, on horseback, on bicycles, by motor lorry, and even in buses quickly commandeered for the purpose.

"What they saw in the hilltop beet field behind the Plough Inn was both impressive and unique," said one account of the event and the scene. "A great tangle of steel bracing wire spread across the grass and tripped up Flying Corps personnel searching for more significant remains. The four Maybach engines lay in different parts of the field, more or less smashed and deeply imbedded in the ground. In the crankcase of one was found a shell-hole, plugged with cotton waste, proving that the airship had been hit before Leefe Robinson gave her the coup de grâce. The control car, which had fallen free, lay completely smashed but untouched by fire."

Off to the side of the field, amid charred fragments of the wooden frame, a large green tarpaulin covered the blackened and mutilated bodies of the officers and crewmen, mostly indistinguishable one from another.

The British splashed recruiting posters all over the country urging people to enlist in the army or navy or join the Home Guard to help fight the monsters who were killing innocent women and children. So great was the response and so significantly did the raids prompt English citizens to enlist in this cause that one German airship officer is said to have commented dourly that he felt as though he had become "a recruiting officer for the British armed forces."

As if this setback were not punishment enough, the Naval Airship Service received a further blow on 16 September when two training ships, *L-6* and *L-9*, caught fire in their dual hangar during inflation when a spark caused by static electricity touched off an explosion in one of the gasbags. The mechanics and operating personnel in the sheds escaped with minor injuries, but the two ships and much of the hangar were completely destroyed.

Despite the slump and his personal fit of depression, Peter Strasser did not give up. He was not a man to sit around brooding over past failures. Within a week he was planning a new series of raids. On 23 September 1916, after waiting for favorable weather and a moonless night, he launched the next big raid, with eight older-type zeppelins dispatched to the Midlands and four of the new superzeppelins headed for London. The latter fleet was under the overall command of Heinrich Mathy, considered the boldest and most enterprising of all of the officers under Strasser's command.

Strasser weighed the choice of going with Peterson, again in *L-32*; with Bocker, who was in command of the newest ship, *L-33*, on her maiden raid; or with Mathy in *L-31*. He elected to go with Mathy, since he might learn some valuable tactical lessons from his greatest, most talented pilot.

Mathy lived up to his billing. Using parachute flares to blind the artillery gunners below as well as to illuminate landforms and structures to check his position, he used the city's railroad tracks as a final guideline to the southern zone of London, which he considered the most weakly defended. From that position he crossed the very center of the city and began unleashing his bombs methodically. In contrast to past raids, the air was strangely free of searchlights and antiaircraft fire because of a fateful break in the weather. Actually, the sector over which *L-31* was flying had been carefully laid out by the British as a zeppelin trap, ringed with guns and searchlights so that no airship could enter and leave without being a sitting duck. However, by phenomenal good luck for the Germans, the Thames was blanketed by heavy mists that blanked out all view of the sky overhead and prevented artillery fire. Similar mists hindered the takeoff of night fighters at Sutton's Farm and other nearby fields so that, by the time the flimsy little planes were airborne and had reached their attack altitudes, the enemy was long since gone.

After dropping almost ten thousand pounds of bombs and inflicting an estimated half a million dollars worth of damage on the city, Mathy sneaked out of the trap by following the fog-shrouded Lea valley. Heading northeast, he totally escaped any significant gunfire or damage as he made his way back to the base at Ahlhorn.

Not until hours later did Mathy and Strasser learn of the major disasters that had marked this ill-fated raid. In *L-33* a less experienced commander, Alois Böcker, followed Mathy's procedure by dropping magnesium parachute flares that blinded the gunners. He also struck boldly at London, coming in over the eastern sector, where he set fire to an oil depot and lumber yards. But he did not have Mathy's good fortune to find a route blanketed by mist and consequently was caught in the glare of searchlights at an altitude of 13,500 feet, well within range of new British guns that had been positioned in strategic locations. A shell burst squarely inside one of *L-33*'s hydrogen cells but for some inexplicable reason did not set the gas afire. The loss of gas, however—accentuated by shrapnel fragments that had punctured other cells—caused the airship to sink at the rate of thirteen feet a second. It was impossible to make repairs and stem the continuing loss of hydrogen.

Böcker ordered full speed, hoping the power of the engines and propellers might help the ship to plane, with nose slightly up, and maintain altitude. But it was no use. The ship continued to lose height as it raced toward the North Sea and the long run home. To complicate matters, a British fighter plane caught up to her and began raking the hull with machine-gun fire until, fortunately for the Germans, the pilot's gun jammed and he had to turn back.

Böcker began jettisoning everything that could possibly be spared, including clothing, guns, ammunition, tools, and reserve fuel. As the airship continued to fall—down to seven hundred feet as the Essex coast appeared in sight—Böcker's last desperate maneuver was simply to crash-land in the water near the shore. The airship did not cooperate with this scheme. With a dying flutter she nosed up and dropped tail-first, settling so gently that the commander and his twenty-one officers and men were able to scramble out unhurt. She was in a pasture near the village of Little Wigborough, not far from a farmhouse and certain to attract immediate attention as soon as daylight arrived.

Böcker's next duty was to destroy the airship so she would not fall into enemy hands. But even in this he was only partially successful. He managed to set fire to the ship's documents and charts by making a puddle of gasoline in the control car, into which he fired a flare. He also set fire to the hydrogen in one of the punctured gas cells. Normally, it would have exploded violently and set fire to the rest of the ship. But the gas simply hissed upward in a bright jet that rapidly diminished and went out. Having no more flares or matches and fearing that the brief blaze would be sighted and soon have the Home Guard on their necks, he decided that he owed it to his men to plan how they might escape.

The strange little band now set out down a country lane, marching boldly along as though it were a unit of the Home

Guard. If they could find public docks, they might be able to steal or commandeer a boat and escape by sea. To the east he could see marshes, and it was in that direction that they headed.

What followed next was a lively little drama of the kind that might only occur in the British countryside. As early dawn cast a pinkish glow to the eastern horizon, they were intercepted by a lone English constable on a bicycle somewhere near Mersea. He did not seem the slightest bit fazed at being outnumbered twenty-two to one and asked them where they thought they were going.

"We are on a special mission," replied Böcker, who spoke flawless English. "Can you tell me how to get to the docks?"

"Never you mind about the docks," the officer replied firmly but politely. "You just come along with me."

Thus ended the war for the officers and men of the Naval Airship Division who later were credited with a unique record: the only Germans to march across British soil during World War I.

As for the wreckage of *L-33*, the British salvaged enough of her to use her as a prototype for the most impressive dirigible ever constructed in England after the war, the ill-fated *R-101*.

The officers and men of *L-32* were not so fortunate. At about midnight commander Werner Peterson began his approach to London on schedule, though more to the east than his orders had specified, along the Thames. Unlike Mathy in *L-31*, he was caught in the glare of numerous searchlights and was a prime target for a multitude of antiaircraft guns that immediately opened fire on him. Although he was above thirteen thousand feet, it was thought that this barrage inflicted some damage and caused him to dump his bombs too hastily and try to escape toward the North Sea.

It was at this moment, shortly before 1:00 A.M., that he was sighted by Second Lieutenant Frederick Sowrey, the same young pilot who had followed Lieutenant William Leefe Robinson into the air on the fateful night when he shot down the *SL-11*. In Sowrey's own words, here is what happened:

At 12:45 A.M., I noticed an enemy airship in an easterly direction. I at once made in this direction and maneuvered into a position underneath. The airship was well lighted by searchlights but there was not any sign of gunfire. I fired at it. The first two drums of ammunition apparently had no effect, but the third one caused the envelope to catch on fire in several places in the center and bow. All firing was traversing fire along the envelope, using drums loaded with a mixture of New Brock, Pomeroy, and tracer ammunition. I watched the burning airship strike the ground and then proceeded to find my flares. I landed at Sutton's Farm at 1:40 A.M., 24th instant. My machine was a BE2c, No. 4112. After seeing the Zeppelin had caught on fire, I fired a red Very light.

The wreckage of *L-32* fell on farmland near the town of Billericay to the northeast of London. It was discovered soon afterward that only one of the crewmen had jumped to his death while the others had stayed with their ship and died in the flames. The crash was particularly rewarding to British Naval Intelligence when one of the searchers found near the wreckage a scorched but still readable copy of the German navy's secret signal book.

The searchers also made another discovery, somewhat unexpected and more unlikely: an icebox from the galley that contained the breakfast the crew had intended to consume on the long flight home, complete with bacon, black bread, and potatoes.

The raid was considered by the British the turning point in zeppelin warfare. The eight German airships that had attacked the Midlands had inflicted very little damage and had apparently found it difficult and frustrating to try to zero in on military targets of any importance. As a report sent to British Intelligence noted, "We used searchlights and artillery posts effectively to discourage the enemy and to place German commanders in situations of stress whereby they had to rush their placements of bombs and did not have time to observe and make decisions about targets and timing. Even without searchlights and anti-aircraft fire, however, it is doubtful that the Zeppelins really have sophisticated enough navigational equipment to locate objectives in the dark of a moonless night. Furthermore, these airships seem to be at the mercy of wind and weather, sometimes drifting where they had not intended to be and at other times getting lost in cloud formations and mists."

The morale level of the German officers and men of the Naval Airship Division would have cheered the British greatly. Even the most outgoing and optimistic airshipmen were brooding about their lot and their inability to bring England to her knees as they had so jubilantly expected a few short months earlier. Their mood was reflected in an account by one of their number, Pitt Klein:

Even in the mess, the old cheerfulness is gone. We discuss our heavy losses, particularly the most recent ones and the crews who will never return. Our nerves are on edge, and even the most energetic and determined cannot shake off the gloomy atmosphere. It is only a question of time before we will join those who have perished before us. Everybody admits that they feel this to be true. Our nerves are made raw by our dismal thoughts. If anyone even dared to claim that he were not haunted by nightmares of burning airships, then he would be labeled a liar. Yet nobody makes such an assertion, each of us having at least the courage to confess our fears.

The commander acts no differently than before, but he has to hide his doubts in the presence of his men and it is only natural that the stress and strain will show in his features and be more deeply etched on his face.

"We will be next, Pitt," taunts our first elevator operator, Quartermaster's Mate Peters.

"You're crazy!" I counter defensively. "We have already made 120 successful battle flights and we serve under the Navy's most outstanding commander. I for one trust our lucky star."

He looks earnestly at me. "Pitt, you know I'm no coward. When we were in eastern Asia, we made many hair-raising voyages through typhoons. Yet I dream constantly of falling Zeppelins. There is something in me that I cannot describe. It is as though there were a strange tunnel of darkness before me into which I am compelled to go."

Kapitänleutnant Heinrich Mathy was no doubt plagued by doubts and fears just as much as Klein, Peters, or any of the other officers and men of the division. Yet he above all was able to camouflage his emotions, in part because he—like his superior, Peter Strasser—still believed that zeppelins could be the undoing of the British. If only their engineers and technicians could devise ways to neutralize incendiary bullets when they struck the gasbags. If only they could perfect navigational equipment to bring them more precisely on target. If only the meteorological stations could predict the weather more accurately. There were just too many ifs, and the only practical way to improve the situation was to upgrade airship training programs and mount more raids so that commanders, navigators, and bombardiers could acquire more experience on the firing line.

With this in mind, he had barely returned from his exceptional run over the center of London than he began lining up men and equipment for another mass raid. As Strasser himself had pointed out, even the presence of airships over British cities, whether they dropped bombs accurately or not, achieved a vital objective. "Every one of those fighter planes sent out against us, every AA battery engaged below us, every man stationed at searchlight controls—these represent enemy forces, equipment, and manpower that the British have to keep at home rather than in France."

France was indeed a critical and highly strategic bone of contention. The battles along the Somme River during the summer of 1916 had required all of France's badly strained resources, along with whatever Great Britain could spare. The French, who had lost heavily in battles at Verdun, had intended to put forty divisions into the Somme attack. Instead, they had to settle for sixteen, since the other twenty-four divisions had been critically depleted by heavy casualties. England, called upon to make up the difference, was hard-pressed to find enough men and equipment to transport to this beleaguered sector in northern France. Here was a case that dramatically proved why bombing raids on England were strategically of far greater importance than the actual amount of damage done to industrial and military targets. If the zeppelin raids could pin down large numbers of men and munitions in England, it would mean the saving of thousands of German lives and guns on the front. The French high command was not happy with the situation and some of its officers were openly critical of the British for diverting so many men and so much armament from the "real" battle on French soil.

Still, to England's credit, the fighting on the ground was described as "preponderantly a British show." When the first battle of the Somme began in early July, the British committed about 185 aircraft for service above the river, along with the infantry troops. They continued feeding planes and troops into the battle (which was to continue into November) through August and in mid-September introduced tanks as well. In the meantime, to the southeast, the French continued to battle furiously to stem the westward-pushing German hordes that were intent on going all the way to Paris. Their losses mounted week after week and right up until mid-December before they were able to slow the German advance and make any significant gains.

The zeppelin commanders were fully aware of these battles and their outcomes and, to some extent at least, attempted to plan bombing raids so that they would negate British plans to send more troops from the homeland to the battlefields of France. Thus it was that on 1 October eleven zeppelins headed once more for England, led by the courageous Mathy in *L-31*. The meteorological station, however, was way off in its forecasts and the supposedly "favorable" weather turned out to be a nightmare for the airship commanders. Five ships lost their bearings completely in sleet and snow, icing up so badly that they were forced to jettison bombs and fuel to maintain altitude and in the end inflicted very little damage.

Mathy, more experienced and resourceful than the others, made a positive landfall near Lowestoft, where he picked up a branch line of the Great Eastern Railway and thus was able to navigate steadily on course to London and avoid some of the bad weather that plagued his peers. But when he reached the outer rim of the city he did not enjoy the luck he had on the earlier raid. He came under heavy fire from ground batteries and was caught by the searchlights long enough and often enough to come under attack by four British fighter planes.

It is evident from reports of observers that Mathy had spotted the planes coming. He dropped all his bombs abruptly, swerved west, and suddenly began to climb, trying to get out of range of both the antiaircraft barrage and the aircraft. But one of the planes, equipped for ultra-high-altitude operation, had reached a height of more than sixteen thousand feet. From this fine vantage point its pilot, Second Lieutenant Wulstan J. Tempest, nosed his plane down, overtook the airship at a very high speed, and opened fire with round after round of incendiary bullets.

Within less than a minute it was all over.

Tempest's report to his superiors, now on record in the Imperial War Museum, vividly recounts the story:

As I drew up to the Zeppelin, to my relief I found that I was free from AA fire for the nearest shells were bursting quite three miles away. The Zeppelin was . . . mounting rapidly. I therefore decided to dive at her, for though I held a slight advantage in speed, she was climbing like a rocket and leaving me standing. I accordingly gave a tremendous pump at my petrol tank [his fuel pump had failed and he was forced to pump the gas by hand] and dived straight at her, firing a burst straight into her as I came. I let her have another burst as I passed under her and then, banking my machine over, sat under her tail and flying along underneath her pumped lead into her for all I was worth.

I could see tracer bullets flying from her in all directions, but I was too close under her for her to concentrate on me. As I was firing, I noticed her begin to glow red inside like an enormous Chinese lantern. Then a flame shot out of the front part of her and I realized she was on fire. She then shot up about 200 feet, hung there momentarily, and came roaring down straight onto me before I had time to get out of the way. I nose-dived for all I was worth, with that Zepp tearing after me, and expected every minute to be engulfed in the flames. I put my machine into a spin and just managed to corkscrew out of the way as she shot down past me, roaring like a furnace.

L-31, like the two sister ships before her, crashed in a field in a London suburb, in this case not far from Cuffley—where *SL-11* had met her fate.

In the sky not far away that night, Peter Strasser rode in the new *L-34*, captained by the very experienced engineer Max Dietrich. At one point he climbed the long ladder up to a gun platform amidships on top of the hull. From there he could survey the overall situation much better than from the control cabin, not blinded by the searchlights below. As *L-34* veered slightly to the north to avoid increasingly heavy AA barrages, he heard exploding bombs to the south and guessed that it must be Mathy in *L-31*: He had vowed that he would give London a pasting such as had never been experienced before.

He wished he had a dozen Mathys. That would give him a huge advantage over the British!

Now, however, he had something else to think about. *L-34* was in trouble, shuddering wildly as artillery shells burst on all sides and the sky around him was licked by searchlights and a new type of flare rocket. Strasser clambered shakily down the ladder and stumbled back along the catwalk to the control gondola, clutching the handrails to keep from being tossed into space. Then, thankfully, Dietrich found a cloud bank to take refuge in and the AA fire immediately dwindled away.

As Strasser reached the gondola he heard one of the crew members shout jubilantly: "A hit! One of our airships has scored a really big hit on London!"

Through occasional rifts in the clouds Strasser could look to the south and see an enormous glow. That was indeed the position that Mathy and *L-31* would have been in, as he had himself observed from the topside machine-gun post. But as he watched the enormous glow on the ground and its counterpart reflected on the clouds overhead, he suddenly felt as though he had been kicked in the stomach. His initial exultation turned into a low moan of anguish. "That was no bomb hit," he said in a low, hoarse voice that could hardly be heard above the drone of the Maybachs. "That was one of our airships."

L-31 had crashed partially against a huge oak, from which many of the branches were stripped and scattered around it a tangled mass of aluminum girders, rising thirty feet or more into the sky like some strange modernist sculpture. As a local villager, one of the first to arrive on the scene, watched the flaming, smoking pyre with feelings of both reverence and disbelief, he noticed something even more unbelievable in a far corner of the field. Approaching, he saw that it was the silhouette of a German officer, clad in uniform and greatcoat and with a muffler tied around his neck. He had either fallen or jumped from the falling ship at a considerable height, for his body was partially imbedded in the soft, moist grass.

The man was still alive, but he died with a final gasp even as the villager attempted to lay him flat and remove the clothing around his throat. The first British officer to reach the scene reached down and removed the military identity disk from around his neck. He let out a cry of astonishment as he read *Kaptlt. Mathy. L-31.*

He stood up and said dumbfoundedly to the small knot of farmers gathered around: "To think that he fell thousands of feet from the sky in the midst of a fireball and lived—even for a few minutes. Why . . . why that's impossible!"

Was it really impossible to survive the crash of a zeppelin on fire, shot down from an altitude of thirteen thousand feet or more? That still remained to be seen, in the strange saga of the *L-48.*

AN INCREDIBLE SURVIVAL

Peter Strasser, often stunned by the deaths of officers and men close to him, was able to hide his feelings and sensitive nature behind the steely military mask he elected to wear. He always wrote letters of condolence to the closest relatives of the officers who lost their lives in the line of duty. In this instance he penned an encomium to the young widow of the friend and fellow officer whose loss would be the most profound in his own personal life:

In the circle of his comrades, his memory will endure as a naval officer such as His Majesty, the Kaiser, revered—daring, tireless, his attention constantly directed toward the enemies of Germany, without consideration for his own personal safety, and at the same time a cheerful, helpful, and true comrade and friend, high in the estimation of his superiors, his equals, and his subordinates.

Now Strasser had to push harder than ever before to obtain approval for new zeppelins for the Naval Airship Division. He might never have done so had he not had the confidence and solid support of Vice Admiral Reinhard von Scheer. Many top-ranking officers, especially in the army, were arguing that better results could be obtained with long-range bombers like the twin-engine Gothas and a four-engine type that was actually being built by the Zeppelin company itself. Some thirty of the giant Gothas had already been ordered by the army, in fact, and would be in service shortly after the new year in 1917. These were faster than zeppelins, could sneak in for an attack at very low altitude, and could not be set on fire or even badly damaged by small planes with incendiary bullets.

Gothas, particularly the later G.IV model, were widely used for attacks on Paris and other cities in France but had enough range to make a number of strategic raids on London, carrying bombs weighing as much as 660 pounds. With 260-horsepower Mercedes engines driving their twin-pusher propellers and with very wide wings, the Gothas could operate at high altitudes and were remarkably nimble for large biplanes. In addition to the bombs, which were slung externally beneath the fuselage, they were well armed for fending off attacking fighter planes. One ingenious part of the design was a "tunnel" through the fuselage that enabled the rear gunner to fire from a position close to the tail, thus giving an unpleasant surprise to enemy pilots who attempted to attack from what was in most aircraft the very vulnerable rear.

Strasser continued pounding home his argument that the damage inflicted on the enemy was only one part of the strategy and that handcuffing huge amounts of enemy military potential was equally important, if not more so. In this he was correct. As the British reported later, by the end of 1916 "there were specifically retained in Great Britain for home antiaircraft defense 17,341 officers and men. There were 12 Royal Flying Corps squadrons, comprising approximately 200 officers, 2,000 men, and 110 aeroplanes. The antiaircraft guns were served by 12,000 officers and men who would have found a ready place, with continuous work, in France or other war theatres."

Strasser also firmly believed that the zeppelins could do far more damage than bombers anyway, that they had greater range, and that all that was really needed now was a new breed of what he referred to as "height-climbers," airships that could climb faster and achieve greater heights, actually out of range of British planes and artillery. He painted a picture of this new zeppelin sitting high in the sky, tantalizingly out of range of circling fighter planes and flak exploding far below.

The aviation department of the Admiralty was already designing a new, more perfectly streamlined engine gondola with a pair of Maybach engines geared to a single superpropeller that was far more efficient than anything previously produced. It was working on the development of an eight-engine airship that was more than seven hundred feet long and could achieve speeds of seventy miles an hour while climbing to ceilings of about thirteen thousand feet. Strasser rejected this design as not suitable for his expectations and indicated that he would be willing to sacrifice some of the speed if the ceilings were increased to just below seventeen thousand feet. This required certain bomb-load sacrifices as well and a general lessening of fuel capacity and ammunition supplies and a lightening of girders, gondolas, and machine-gun positions.

Although improvements in zeppelin design had gradually made the airships capable of climbing to higher and higher

111

altitudes, the use of oxygen had been spotty—sometimes because commanders had not expected to have to push their craft to the heights they did. But now Strasser fully acknowledged that his plan required the addition of oxygen supplies and masks for the crew and was among the first to test the various kinds of equipment then available. When the first height climber, *L-42*, was delivered, Strasser accompanied it on its test flight, rising to the unprecedented height of almost twenty thousand feet. The design of this ship incorporated fundamental recommendations made by Machinist's Mate Adolf Schultz, who had been aboard *L-33* when she crash-landed in Essex and had been recently repatriated in a prisoner exchange from England to Switzerland. Schultz, referring to the heavy losses in 1916, recommended that ships be capable of attaining altitudes above nineteen thousand feet if they expected to survive attacks over England.

A great deal of military—and political—maneuvering took place during the development of the 40-class height climbers, but Strasser pushed his program and these ships went from the drawing board into production. The new *L-40*, which arrived in January 1917, could operate smoothly at more than seventeen thousand feet. *L-42*, which made its test flight with Strasser aboard in March, climbed to more than nineteen thousand five hundred feet and could have gone higher after dropping her bomb load (represented simply by water ballast on this occasion).

One of the new ships delivered in the spring of 1917 was *L-48*, which had a new kind of control gondola that was some twenty-five hundred pounds lighter than that of her previously produced sister ship and had other improvements making her fully fit for a new wave of raids that were expected to give the British an unpleasant surprise. In mid-June she was ready for her first raid, but the British did not yet know about her and her supposed invincible capabilities. She would be to them just another raider.

★ ★ ★

It was warm and clear over the coast of England the evening of 16 June 1917. At the makeshift airstrip, bumpy and rough-turfed at Orford Ness, 125 miles northwest of London, Captain Robert Saundby, Royal Flying Corps, sat on a wooden bench outside the small frame-and-canvas hangar, chewing the end of a dead cigar. "Maybe you chaps will have your first go tonight," he said to two new pilots. "Looks like zepp weather."

"It does, Sir," they agreed. They had just been transferred to Saundby's squadron with two planes especially equipped for attacking airships at night. "We're ready any time."

Saundby grunted, trying to relight his butt. He was hardly optimistic about the chances of either of the fragile little planes that squatted, petrol tanks full and machine guns loaded with incendiaries, at the takeoff line. It was true that the Royal Flying Corps had shot down six zeppelins in less than a year, but two of the airships had been old models and the other four had been caught by surprise when venturing in at too low an altitude. Now the Germans had a big, new breed of zeppelin that could outclimb the best of the British night fighters.

At 11:00 P.M. Saundby slid his lanky frame off the bench and headed for the officers' quarters. "Well, I'm calling it a night," he said with a sigh of boredom. "If there's any excitement, let me know. I could use some."

Saundby had reason to be bored. He had only recently returned from the front, having flown several hundred hours of combat time. Just a year earlier he had been in the thick of the battles of the Somme as the Allies tried to wrest air superiority from the vicious little Fokker monoplanes. Now, with the first American troops pouring into France, he was relegated to the dismal quiet of Orford Ness, where life was about as exciting as milking cows and gathering hay. Even *suspense* was lacking.

In the first five and a half months of 1917 there had been only one zeppelin raid anywhere near the area. And then the clouds had been so dense that the zeppelins had flown at seventeen thousand feet, unseen and completely out of reach of either aircraft or artillery. Life with the Home Defense was dull; but, of course, there was always the thought that rumors about the new German superzeppelins *might* be true.

"We need you *here*, on the English coast, more than we need your experience at the front," the colonel at the Air Office had told him. "Intelligence tells us that the Jerries have really done it—perfected zepps that will climb to twenty thousand feet and deliver almost four tons of high explosives apiece."

Captain Saundby went off to bed, confident that no superzeppelins were likely to disturb his sleep that night.

Around noon that same day, however—16 June—an event that would have interested Captain Robert Saundby, RFC, had taken place. In the great zeppelin shed at Nordholz, Germany, Kapitänleutnant Otto Mieth paced nervously back and forth on the hardcaked earth floor, eyeing first one engine gondola, then another on the giant zeppelin *L-48*, whose monstrous bag stretched almost seven hundred feet.

"Hurry up, Ellermann!" he called to the chief engineer, who seemed to be having trouble with a fuel pump in the starboard aft gondola. "We have to be airborne by one o'clock."

Mieth was nervous. *L-48* was the newest and one of the best of airships, ready to take off on her first war mission. As a junior officer, Mieth was not only responsible to his skipper, Kapitänleutnant Franz Georg Eichler, but on this mission would also be under the eye of Korvettenkapitän★ Victor Schütze. Schütze, commodore of the North Sea Airship Division, was second only to Fregatenkapitän Peter Strasser, the tough, intense man who

---

★ Lieutenant commander.

had already made it clear that "on this flight there can be no failure."

As the minutes passed Mieth's pace increased. His mouth hungered for the taste of a cigarette—a pleasure denied members of the zeppelin service while on duty, under penalty of death. A single spark could, in a matter of seconds, touch off thousands of cubic feet of highly flammable hydrogen gas and reduce the ugly giant to nothing but twisted aluminum girders and ashes.

"We are ready, Lieutenant," said chief engineer Heinz Ellermann at last. His assurance came seconds before the shed echoed with the raucous sound of a Klaxon, the signal that Oberleutnant Eichler had ordered L-48 to move out of the hangar.

Now the Nordholz shed was bedlam as one engine after another coughed into motion amid shouts of "Contact!" . . . "Mind the propeller!" . . . "Clutch in!" In the background Mieth could hear the jangle of telegraph bells in the pilot gondola of the airship as each engineman signaled to the navigator that he was ready.

Two officers with gold braid on their flight caps and sleeves approached the airship and swung themselves up into the control gondola: Eichler and Schütze.

"All clear for leaving the shed!" shouted the ground officer from a vantage point at the huge open doors of the shed, where he could keep an eye on the wind sock.

"Airships Ma-a-a-a-rch!" Mieth barked the order to the ground crews, then swung himself up into the gondola, near his two senior officers.

Slowly the zeppelin eased out of the hangar. A slight wind tugged at L-48's nose as she poked through the door, but the airship was kept straight by the ground crew and by trolleys running from the gondola to tracks embedded in the shed floor. Mieth now saw that it was a perfect June day, with gentle breezes and a few cumulus clouds overhead.

All at once there was a sharp crack, like a whip snapping overhead. Tense eyes jerked upward.

"It is nothing," said Schütze icily. "A bit of the skin has cracked because of the sudden heat of the midday sun."

"I don't like it," muttered Ellermann in the starboard gondola. Like many other members of the crew, he was a former sailor, recruited from the ranks at the beginning of the war when the German Naval Airship Service was born. And a good seaman was always superstitious.

Of the four zeppelins leaving Nordholz that afternoon, *L-48* was the last to get into the air. Some five hundred yards out of the shed, with ground crews holding tightly onto the guide ropes, the ship's five 250-horsepower Maybach engines were clutched in.

"Stand by for ascent!" shouted Eichler, quickly following with the command "Up bow!" The bow of the gondola was instantly released and the big, blunt nose tilted into the blue of the sky.

"Up stern!" The ground crew aft let go, and the entire ship was airborne.

Mieth glanced at his watch. It was exactly 1:15 P.M. Ahead he could see, two or three miles distant, the dark shapes of three other zeppelins against the blue sky: The nearest was *L-42*, under the command of Kapitänleutnant Martin Dietrich. "Due north" he could hear Eichler ordering the helmsman. "Our first bearing is Helgoland."

Now, safely and steadily aloft, the twenty-one officers and men aboard *L-48* settled down to the routine of crossing the North Sea to deliver the three tons of bombs slung under the zeppelin's belly.

Kapitänleutnant Mieth stood watch as *L-48* droned northwest toward England at sixty knots. Though the afternoon remained fair, he noted that a considerable headwind had sprung up so that by six o'clock forward speed had been substantially reduced. To relieve the monotony of flight, Mieth climbed up into the bag, balanced his way along the catwalk, and then scrambled down into the starboard gondola aft, to check on engine performance.

"No trouble, Sir," reported engineer Heinz Ellermann. "We can give you plenty more power anytime—if the wind continues rising."

Ellermann was a quiet man with a girlfriend whom he had been about to visit on two weeks' leave when his orders were suddenly changed to include the June sixteenth mission. He was lonely, thought Mieth, and scared—perched by himself where there was nothing to do but think of the oncoming night and the many zeppelins on former raids that had ended their careers as funeral pyres, plummeting from the English sky.

Finally, Mieth scrambled dizzily back to his post in the control gondola. The altitude was affecting him now. As he came down the ladder he saw the captain bending over the charts with Schütze. "We are approaching the Suffolk coast," said Eichler.

That accounted for Mieth's dizziness. The ship had climbed to fifteen thousand feet and was still rising in anticipation of the British antiaircraft guns and planes.

By now the late sunset was coloring the cumulus clouds an eerie blood-red. Mieth had a strange sensation that the sky was filled, in the west, with dozens of strange, grotesque airships of another day and age. Then darkness began to settle in as the fleet droned on. For a while, not far ahead, he could make out the silhouette of *L-42*. Then she, too, disappeared, and *L-48* was alone, now at seventeen thousand feet in a bitterly cold sky.

If he only could have some oxygen, Mieth thought. But the precious oxygen had to be saved for that critical time when the zeppelin would have to rise to eighteen thousand feet . . . twenty thousand feet . . . to escape the deadly reach of the enemy.

★   ★   ★

117

If the Germans were having it hard, the British were experiencing an agony of a different sort.

All along the Suffolk coast, down into Essex, and up the Thames to London, the citizens of southeastern England were tense and expectant. During raids in March and May 1917 the zeppelins had done little damage. But their aim had been obscured by heavy layers of cloud. Tonight, the June sky was clear.

"Those new superzepps," a Home Defense guard at Ipswich had said, "can sit up there, more than three miles high, and pick out targets below, like a small boy on a bridge dropping rocks on the ducks. And who can do anything about it?"

At about 11:15 P.M., when the air-raid sirens, bells, and Klaxons began to set up their weird cacophony from the Dover coast north to The Wash, civilians were certain that, finally, this was the moment of disaster. The long-expected supermonsters of Fregatenkapitän Peter Strasser finally were a reality. Now, all of the rumors of the past months were snowballed into one great sphere of terror, which rolled across the English countryside. Some said that the Germans had long possessed diabolic super-zeppelins and were only now resorting to this inhuman form of warfare because the Americans had finally landed in France.

At 11:35, the keeper aboard the Haisboro lightship, some ten miles at sea, reported hearing the deep throb of engines to the east. Three minutes later he described "a great, dark shape almost directly overhead—bigger than any zeppelin I ever saw." This was *L-48*.

To the south, directly east of the mouth of the Thames, another lightship sent a similar report by radio. Then, for about an hour, there was nothing—no sound, no dark shapes, no bombs—as the English waited tensely in the night.

★   ★   ★

Captain Robert Saundby, commander of the little RFC squadron at Orford Ness, had barely gotten his pajamas on at eleven-fifteen the night of 16 June when he heard running footsteps on the ground outside, followed by a knock on his door.

"Raid, Sir! Zeppelin raid!" It was the voice of his orderly.

"Right," Saundby said. "I'll be dressed directly. Sound the alert." He could hear the far-off sounds of a church bell to the west, at Orford or Woodbridge. Then a plane engine coughed as a mechanic began spinning the prop on the BE2c. A minute later it was repeated, this time on the FE2b. Then silence.

The next sounds, as he strode toward the takeoff point, were streams of swear words as the two pilots fumbled with switches and gear in their eagerness to get their machines aloft.

"Take it easy, lads," said Saundby. "I don't want you to go up until I get a report from the Colonel."

"But, Sir, it will take us almost an hour to climb to thirteen thousand feet. That's the lowest altitude one of those flying sausages would possibly risk."

"I know, I know. Warm your engines."

More turning of props. More swearing. Finally, the protesting chatter of the engines, rising and falling. Saundby spent the next ten minutes on and off the phone. When he received the report passed along from the Haisboro lightship, he decided that it was time for action. He ordered his small force into the air.

There was the sound of "Chocks away!" Then the two flimsy little ships bounced down the rough airstrip, racing each other to be the first to climb up into the dark, cool sky.

When they were out of sight, Saundby strolled to a wooden bench in front of the canvas hangar and lay down on his back, palms under his head. War seemed so utterly remote and unreal to him as he gazed, straight upward at the stars.

★　★　★

"Kapitän, the coast!"

At exactly midnight the helmsman in the control gondola of
L-48 picked out, some seventeen thousand feet below, the dark
shape of the Suffolk shoreline. Ten minutes later, with the coast
almost directly beneath, Eichler ordered the ship to follow it
south, then north, while the navigator picked out distinguish-
ing features so he could identify his position exactly on the
chart.

At 12:45, having determined that the airship was slightly north
of the river Deben, Oberleutnant Eichler decided to head directly
west about fifteen miles and bomb some industrial plants located
in the city of Ipswich.

"Break out oxygen," he ordered.

For the next fifteen minutes *L-48* zigzagged offshore, maintaining her position while preparations were made for the bombing run. During all of the action, Korvettenkapitän Victor
Schütze patiently remained an official observer. Despite his ele-
vated rank, he gave no orders to Eichler.

Kapitänleutnant Otto Mieth was assigned by Eichler to the
radio room, a cramped cubicle in the rear of the control gondola,
to intercept any messages from the British that might reveal they
were over a vital target or to pick up weather information that
would be of use on the return trip.

Now they could see British searchlights inland and hear the
echo of antiaircraft fire. These actions made them wonder
whether any, or all, of the other three ships on the raid had swung
in over targets.

In the noisy little aft starboard engine gondola, engineer Heinz
Ellermann saw the searchlights, though he could not hear the
artillery blasts. He felt a great desire to cut off the engines. If *L-48*
could just drift silently, like a huge balloon in the midnight sky,
she could not be detected by the British listening posts. The posts

were equipped with a new type of orthophone, great trumpet-shaped "ears" that could pick up the sound of approaching engines at considerable distance.

Ellermann took a drag on the oxygen tube and wished the ship would climb higher. He did not know the latest range of the British AA guns or the ceiling for the new night fighters he had heard about. All he did know for certain was that seventeen thousand feet did not seem nearly high enough and that when the ship finally did go in over a target, Eichler would probably descend another two thousand feet or more to make sure of his hits. He could not help thinking now of his girl and the fact that, had his orders not been changed, he would probably at that very moment be holding her in his arms in the warm June night beside a lake, or drinking good wine and dancing in a beergarden in Bremen. It made him more afraid than ever that he might die. There never were survivors when an airship went down in flames from accident, artillery burst, or—in recent months—the incendiary bullets of fighter planes. *No survivors!*

Suddenly, there was a sharp glare of light and *L-48* was caught momentarily by a searchlight as she headed inland for the Harwich–Ipswich area and her targets. Then the finger of light swept past as the British searchlight crew lost the high-flying zeppelin again.

Captain Robert Saundby stirred restlessly on the hard wooden bench outside the canvas hangar at Orford Ness, waking up from a fitful catnap. He opened his eyes and glanced at his watch. The luminous hands indicated a few minutes before 1:00 A.M. In the distance he could hear the sound of aircraft engines.

"They shouldn't be back yet," he muttered to himself, thinking that the BE2c and the FE2b might be returning from their patrol. He swung his eyes in an arc across the sky, then suddenly froze. There, painted white by searchlights about ten miles away, was the stark shape of a zeppelin.

"My God!" Saundby dashed into the hangar, where two of his mechanics were sleeping on cots, fully dressed, awaiting the return of the patrol planes. "Zeppelin!" he shouted. "Let's get *Debbie* out—on the double!"

The startled grease monkeys leaped as though they had been prodded with a red-hot poker. Within two minutes they had Saundby's single-seater DH2 fighter out of the hangar—a pusher type, equipped only for daylight duels with German Fokkers. She had no navigation lights, no dashboard lights, and only the simplest flying instruments: altimeter, airspeed indicator, and bubble. Saundby had never flown at night in his life. But the sky was clear; he knew his ship had enough petrol for at least three hours of flight—enough to keep him aloft until early dawn—and he was determined now to have a close look at one of these German monsters, to see how terrifying they really were.

"Switch on."

"Contact." The mechanic swung the propeller with a frantic heave. The engine coughed, died, caught, and roared into life.

Saundby could feel the little ship shaking like a leaf in a high wind as he revved the engine furiously, much too fast, eager to get rolling.

"Chocks away!" The DH2 leaped forward, bouncing over the rough turf as the pilot coaxed her faster and faster. Then she was in the air and climbing swiftly into the cool, clear night.

Saundby headed toward the position where he had last seen the zepp, figuring that it would take him about half an hour to reach the location and the altitude. But after fifteen minutes of flying he saw the zeppelin suddenly, caught by a crisscross of searchlights and looking as though someone had lit an elongated Japanese lantern in the heavens. Within seconds after she was spotted, antiaircraft shells began bursting in the air but at least three thousand feet below the airship. Saundby felt a surge of disappointment. The zeppelin was probably far, far beyond his fighter plane's ceiling, which was not more than fifteen thousand feet.

For the next hour Saundby pushed his machine upward into the night, trying vainly to get high enough. The zeppelin was now almost constantly in the glare of searchlights, but her crew seemed entirely unconcerned. She zigzagged slowly, out of range of both planes and antiaircraft fire, looking for her targets.

Far to the south Saundby could hear the sound of something other than AA bursts: the explosion of bombs. *L-42* had made a run in over the southeastern tip of England and was bombing Ramsgate. Then the explosions sounded much closer, and Saundby realized that the zeppelin he was trailing was also unloading bombs somewhere to the north of Harwich. He was slightly over fourteen thousand feet, circling the zeppelin, unable to go in closer because of the heavy AA fire and the airship's greater altitude. He wondered where the other two planes of his squadron had gone. By 3:00 A.M. he had followed the zeppelin in a great circle, heading north and almost over his own airfield again. He began to be concerned about the amount of fuel left in his tank, but he had noted with some relief that he was able to make out landmarks below—the coastline and an occasional river or pond.

He was about ready to call it quits. The zeppelin had apparently delivered all of her bombs and was headed northeast, probably to swing out to sea in a sector where no British warships could get a range on her. It was bitterly disappointing to Saundby, but he decided to keep the airship in sight until his tanks held barely enough fuel for the return trip to his airfield.

In the control gondola of *L-48* as the airship approached Harwich, everything was functioning with the utmost precision. At first the searchlights had disconcerted everyone—even the steely-faced Korvettenkapitän Victor Schütze. Then, when it was seen that the antiaircraft fire was continuously short of range, the officers and men relaxed and concentrated on trying to locate the targets.

At 2:40 *L-48* unloaded two high-explosive bombs about five miles east of Ipswich. Ten minutes later she dropped five more on what the navigator ascertained to be an industrial plant on the banks of the Deben. On both runs Eichler also ordered incendiaries released. He could not determine how much damage was done, but as the ship swung northward again, parts of the British countryside could be seen blazing away.

In between the two runs, the tail gunner and one of the enginemen reported seeing the shape and the exhaust of at least one fighter plane, possibly two. The enemy, however, was far below. Eichler knew that unless German Intelligence was slipping badly, there was not a British fighter in existence that could outclimb a zeppelin in the new L-40 class.

"Due north," he ordered the helmsman.

At 3:00 A.M. Kapitänleutnant Otto Mieth, enclosed in the tiny radio cubicle, picked up a wireless message from part of the German fleet in the North Sea. One of the observation airships accompanying the fleet reported a good wind from the west at thirteen thousand feet. It would blow the airship along nicely on the return flight to Nordholz. And, since dawn would start to break within the hour, it would be wise to make haste for home. He reported the message to Oberleutnant Eichler.

"Valve gas," ordered the commander. "Bring her down to thirteen thousand. Hold course."

The men at the controls tilted the nose down slightly, and the great shape of the *L-48* slid from seventeen thousand feet downward in an easy glide. The zeppelin's engines droned smoothly on. The ship had reached an altitude of about fourteen thousand feet when suddenly Ahrens, the stoker petty officer, who had been gazing aft from the control car into the darkness, let out a shout of warning.

"Plane! Fighter plane, approaching fast from behind! Port side, about five hundred feet below us!"

"Climb, climb! Heave ballast. Emergency!" Eichler said. He gave the order that every zeppelin man dreaded, knowing that it meant that they were under attack. The airship lurched suddenly upward as several hundred pounds of ballast were released and the bow, simultaneously, tilted skyward.

About 3.10 A.M., with a pale streak of dawn already visible to the east, Captain Robert Saundby was still following the zeppelin northward. Her great shape was clearly visible against the sky, ahead and about three thousand feet above him, well out of machine-gun range. He was about to give up and return to his base when he sensed a change in the relative positions of plane and airship. He could not be sure, but the zeppelin's nose seemed to be inclining *downward*.

By 3:15 there was no doubt about it. The zeppelin was, for some reason, losing altitude. Saundby gave the DH2 full throttle and tried once more to climb. It was impossible to tell whether the plane was responding, but it was evident that the airship was descending closer and closer. He swung off to the left of the ship slightly, planning to fly in a slight arc so that he could attack amidships, with the whole broad expanse of the airship's gasbag in front of him.

Then, all at once, he saw the airship's nose tilt upward. He had been spotted. It was now or never!

Saundby tilted his gun to an angle of forty degrees and pressed the trip. He figured his range at about one thousand feet as he let loose a double drum of incendiary bullets. Now, from somewhere atop the dark bag of *L-48*, a machine gun was chattering away. He could see tracers coming toward him but far wide of the mark.

Quickly Saundby loaded more drums and fired. Nothing happened, not even after he had used up seven. The zeppelin was climbing fast now, almost out of range. Saundby jammed his eighth and last drum of incendiaries into the housing and tripped his guns. This time, he was successful. He found his mark and within a matter of seconds, there could be no doubt that the zeppelin had become the latest victim of aerial attack by the Royal Flying Corps. Saundby had witnessed many fires in his lifetime, but nothing that could compare with the explosion of flame as this huge mass of hydrogen lit the entire sky. He wondered momentarily what it must have looked like from the ground as the city's defenders looked up into what had, until then, been a totally black sky.

Perched in the front of the DH2 with the pusher engine behind him, Saundby caught the surge of heat that suddenly replaced the cold night air. For a moment he thought that he, too, had been engulfed in the fire. The plane wobbled crazily, like a rowboat caught by breakers. It started to spin, and Saundby found all his efforts devoted to keeping control of his craft and trying to sideslip away from the fiery demon in the sky.

Then it was all over. He was circling through the cold sky again and two thousand feet below, a seven-hundred-foot-long fireball was plummeting the remaining twelve thousand feet to earth, trailing a great pillar of smoke and flames.

Poor devils! Poor, poor devils! Saundby covered his eyes with one hand as the shock of it all hit him. He was shaking violently, his initial jubilance at having scored a hit smothered in the wave of anguish that came from seeing how violently men could die.

For perhaps ten minutes he circled numbly over the spot at Westleton where *L-48* had gone down, hypnotized by the sight below. The debris was still burning brightly as Saundby throttled down and descended gradually southward toward the little field at Orford Ness.

Aboard *L-48* when the plane was sighted, Kapitänleutnant Otto Mieth's first impression that something was wrong came when he was abruptly hurled backward against the after wall of the tiny radio compartment. With earphones on, he had not heard the warning cry outside. But there could be no doubt about why *L-48*'s elevators had been frantically swung to push the nose skyward again.

Mieth remained at his post during the exchange of machine-gun fire. Then it died away and he thought to himself, perhaps we are clear now and out of range.

Mieth's next sensation was that the entire airship had been rocked by a tremendous wall of air—the kind of phenomenon that happened when a zeppelin was caught in a thunderstorm, except much greater. Even with the earphones on he could hear an enormous explosion. Then the tail began to settle. With the ship at a forty-five-degree angle, bow to stern, he was half-lying against the rear wall of the radio compartment. Outside, against the front wall, he could hear equipment crashing and sliding down, then the thump of bodies as Eichler, Schütze, and the others in the outer part of the control gondola fell against the bulkheads.

Down, down the airship plunged now, stern first. Mieth could hear a tremendous whistling sound, punctuated by occasional small explosions as gas tanks were touched off. The heat was growing intense, and he felt as though he were being baked alive in the radio compartment that had turned into an oven. Outside he could hear the cries of agony as the men died the horrible death of being incinerated.

Schütze's voice rose above them. It was loud, clear, and as icily calm as though he were bringing his ship in for a landing: "In a moment, it will be all over!"

Mieth tried to pull the hood of his flight jacket around his face, to cut out the sharp stabs of heat that seemed to be roasting his face. In a moment of great calm, he found himself wondering whether he could possibly push the compartment door open, get past the bodies jammed around it, and dive from the falling airship.

Mieth was heaving against the door when he heard a splintering, shattering sound behind him. The tail of the flaming skeleton had hit the ground in a cornfield at a place named Holly Tree Farm. The control gondola was flipped violently sideways by the impact, away from the rest of the ship. Something struck him against the thighs and he felt the sharp agony of bones breaking. Then the pain swelled up all over him and he was engulfed by the black relief of unconsciousness.

Kapitänleutnant Otto Mieth survived the crash and eventually recovered, although both thighs were broken and he was severely burned. He awoke the next morning in a British hospital to hear an English voice asking him, "Do you want a cigarette?"

Incredible though Mieth's survival was, he was not the only man to live through it. Engineer Heinz Ellermann was the other of the only two men who ever survived the crash of a zeppelin shot down in flames. "The ship was crashing at a terrific rate," he wrote later, "and the air whistled as she cut her way through it . . . the gasbags were burning away like mad . . . a frizzling sound just like a bit of greasy paper has when you throw it on the fire. The draft was driving the flames to port. I was in the starboard walkway, but all the same, I felt the heat through to my leggings. I tried to beat out the flames on my fur coat, but a sleeve caught fire. The ship was falling, falling, falling. . . . Suddenly the ship's stern crashed to pieces with a fearful din. I only knew that a chaotic jumble of girders, bracing wires, benzine tanks and car fittings were coming down on my head, and that above me a sea of flames was collapsing. 'Now keep your head,' I thought, 'and don't lose your breath.' "

Ellermann could never forget those seconds that seemed like an eternity. But he did manage to hold his breath and not inhale any of the flames or deadly fumes.

"My fur coat was burning on my back. I was imprisoned in a cage, the bars of which were a glowing, red-hot mass. With all my strength, I pushed against a girder. Another girder gave way in front of me and left a gap free. I crawled along the ground and felt grass. I crept forward. Behind me was a mass of burning oil. I rolled over two or three times in the grass. Then I found myself in the open air. Ten feet away from some burning debris, I collapsed."

For Germany, the tragedy of the *L-48* was more of a blow than what had become almost routine, the loss of an airship and the death of nineteen officers and men. It was an ominous sign that the zeppelin was not going to be the weapon that would win the war. Ironically, Kapitänleutnant Mieth's escape from death, while a miracle of survival, was also an unintended instrument for demoralizing his fellow officers and men of the Naval Airship Division. In a letter smuggled out of an Allied prison camp he described the *L-48*'s tragic flight and flaming demise and the circumstances surrounding the zeppelin's encounter with the little British fighter plane that fateful June night, one part of which asserted his opinions:

"The zeppelin is doomed. The British fighter pilots now have machines with both greatly increased altitude capabilities and longer range. Furthermore, they seem to have a new incendiary bullet that cannot fail."

From the time his prison letter was received by his German compatriots until the end of the war no airship crew headed out across the North Sea without Mieth's ominous prediction in mind: "The zeppelin is doomed."

PAYING THE PRICE

T he height-climber zeppelins achieved one major objective in that they were able to operate well out of range of the existing antiaircraft guns and most of the fighter planes from the spring of 1917 until the end of the war. And, during the raids that followed, the British often could do nothing but watch, grinding their teeth and knowing that defense technology would never catch up, even with massive technological research and the expenditure of vast sums of money they did not have in their coffers anyway.

The high-altitude characteristics of the new airships, however, exacted a heavy price of the Germans. Cruising at altitudes over

ten thousand feet made navigation more complicated and difficult, especially when there were many moving cloud formations
below. Navigators became more and more dependent on radio
signals to stay on course, but the bearings were usually unreliable
at best and any use of wireless involved signals that immediately
alerted the British defenders and helped them zero in on approaching raiders.

When airships reached altitudes of thirteen thousand feet and
more they frequently experienced engine trouble because of the
lack of the oxygen necessary to make the fuel burn efficiently. In
many cases, extreme cold and icing were also problems that
plagued the mechanics as they tried to keep their engines from
freezing up. There was no way the power engineers could design
engines that would function properly near ground level where
the summer afternoon temperatures might be in the eighties at
the start of the flights and then drop during the night at very
high altitudes to as low as ten or twenty degrees below zero Fahr-
enheit.

Mechanical breakdowns affected every part of the ship: not
just the engines, but fabric that became so brittle it would break,
celluloid windows that shattered, control cables that refused to
budge, and instruments containing fluids or lubricants that froze
and rendered the components useless.

Even worse, the physiological effect on officers and men was
devastating. As many as two dozen mysterious deaths were later
attributed to a form of heart failure caused by the combination of
cold and lack of oxygen. Several men died when their primitive
oxygen masks failed while they were in isolated positions such as
machine-gun posts atop the airship and they lost consciousness
long before their comrades found them and could revive them.

Altitude sickness was common and severe, sometimes rendering entire crews unfit for duty for a week or more after a high-

flying raid. Dizziness, severe headaches, nausea, and vomiting were common early warnings of this malady. On at least three occasions, zeppelins wandered far off course before officers on board realized that their navigators (and in one case the commander) were only semiconscious and thus completely incapable of making any rational decisions. It was later discovered that the oils and chemicals used in the primitive breathing apparatuses issued to the crew so severely contaminated the oxygen that these victims had literally been poisoned.

A German medical officer described the confusion in the ranks of his compatriots when they were asked to determine the physiological problems and advise the Naval Airship Division on methods to counter altitude sickness. This form of illness had been so little anticipated that no research had been undertaken at that time. An account by one of the medical officers at the Ahlhorn base shed some light on the problem: "Above 13,000 feet we see signs of the now familiar altitude symptoms, which manifest themselves as dizziness, ringing in the ears, and headaches. At greater heights, a marked acceleration of respiration and cardiac activity takes place. Pulse rates of 120 to 150 per minute are by no means uncommon. These severe imbalances can be controlled only by the continuous inhalation of oxygen from masks."

He added some comments about the ingestion of food and liquids at high altitudes, concluding that chocolate was one of the few kinds of nourishment that could safely be consumed and that crews were better off not to eat even the lightest meals at high altitudes.

Medical researchers were hard pressed to come up with antidotes for other problems induced by high altitudes such as frostbite, muscular cramps, stiff joints, and severely cracked lips. Attempts were made to design clothing that would prevent such problems, but invariably the solutions were such that they added intolerable amounts of weight or hindered and restricted the crews from performing necessary duties in flight. Another enormous problem was fatigue, which was aggravated greatly by both the low temperatures and the thin air as well as by the fact that it was too cold for a crewman to lie in a hammock and hope to get any sleep.

Even the usually optimistic and energetic Peter Strasser was depressed by the problems. He had expected great things of the new high-climbers and he could not shake from his mind the unexpected tragedy and loss of *L-48*. When he read Otto Mieth's account of the disaster, smuggled out of his prison camp, it was as though he himself had been in that flaming control gondola.

> Our vast ship was a pillar of fire [Mieth had written]. You could see her aluminum skeleton slowly peel itself out of the fire, and the acrid smell of burning came right into our gondola. So this is death! I thought. My God, when it's so near it's terrible. I called out to Schütze, "Captain, take off your coat because we are coming right down on water." But Schütze stood there without moving a muscle. He looked up toward the flames and serenely awaited death. His voice did not shake when he said to the others, "In a moment it will all be over."

And so, a brave man, Strasser's second-in-command, had met his end. He would not by any means be the last to do so.

For a few months Strasser virtually decided that he would completely change Naval Airship Division strategy. He would call off, or at least minimize, high-flying raids until some of the problems of altitude and extreme cold could be solved or at least alleviated. He had good reason and what seemed a significant strategic alternative. The German high command, after being

134

suppressed for two years from mounting unrestricted submarine warfare, had won the Kaiser's approval in late winter 1917 to let the U-boats go all-out against Allied shipping. Wilhelm II had been talked into believing that England could be dealt a headlock that would bring about a plea for peace negotiations before the end of the year.

At the beginning of the war, German submarines had proved their value as strategic weapons by sinking a British cruiser, the *Aboukir*, off the Dutch coast and later the warships *Hogue* and *Cressy*, which went to the bottom with nearly all hands. During the Dardanelles campaign against Turkey, the British had lost the battleships *Triumph* and *Majestic* to German U-boats. Later in the war, however, and especially after the sinking of the *Lusitania* by the *U-20*, with its heavy loss of civilian passengers, the sentiment of neutral nations turned against Germany. As a result, the German high command was split by controversy. Navy minister Admiral Alfred von Tirpitz argued that unrestricted submarine warfare was the only way in which the Germans could overcome British naval superiority. Chancellor Theobald von Bethmann-Holweg took the opposite stand, arguing that U-boat sinkings would eventually draw America into the war on the side of the Allies.

"Our fleet has become the hilt of the sword whose sharp blade is the submarine," asserted Fleet Admiral Reinhard von Scheer as the undersea assault on the British got under way. His words rang true when, in February 1918 alone, the Allies lost more than 780,000 tons of shipping to submarine torpedoes. Since von Scheer badly needed eyes for his growing undersea fleet, to detect mines, sight targets, and to warn against other countermeasures by British submarines and other units of the Royal Navy, zeppelins were a ready answer. They had served well in the past and could undertake greatly stepped-up operations now.

At first, airships were dispatched on scouting missions over the

North Sea with the German fleet at the same altitudes they had been ordered to maintain on bombing runs over London and the Midlands: no less than thirteen thousand feet. At such heights, however, they were unable to spot mines or enemy submarines and found it difficult even to identify large warships. So Strasser countered by permitting his commanders to patrol at considerably lower altitudes—at which, indeed, they were able to do the job intended.

On 21 August 1917, in daylight with scattered clouds, *L-23* was well out over the North Sea with no sign of trouble. She had spotted and identified the British light cruiser *Yarmouth* engaged in a mine-laying operation. Remaining at about eight thousand feet, well out of range of the British naval guns, she was easily able to report every detail of the enemy's maneuvers by wireless to the German fleet.

What the German observers missed, however, was some unprecedented activity at the forward end of the cruiser as she swung into the wind. There, from a small platform affixed to the bow, the British launched a Sopwith Pup. Flight Sublieutenant B. A. Smart, who had never before flown his plane off a ship, got aloft on the steady breeze without any mishap. He was not even spotted by the zeppelin observers as he streaked along the choppy waters, then circled and climbed to an altitude of about nine thousand feet. From that vantage point he dived to within a hundred feet of the zeppelin's hull and opened fire with incendiary bullets.

Just before plunging to the sea in flames, *L-23* was able to transmit a final message: "Pursued by enemy forces."

According to the procedure the British had decided upon, Lieutenant Smart crash-landed his Sopwith on the water alongside a destroyer and was plucked from the waves unhurt. As for the zeppelin, there was nothing of any value or significance left to fish from the oil-streaked surface where she had gone down.

This new disaster and the arrival in England of a supply of long-range Curtiss flying boats from the United States effectively spelled the end of the zeppelin fleet-observation operations.

On that same day Peter Strasser was also out on a mission, leading a fleet of eight zeppelins in a raid on England. On this occasion, though, it was the turn of the British to do the sweating. The Fregatenkapitän maintained his formation at close to twenty thousand feet during the entire attack—an altitude that rendered England's fighter planes and antiaircraft guns completely useless. The raid accomplished its intended purpose, and in addition made the enemy feel more uncomfortable than ever.

Strasser had another opponent to contend with now. Many officers in both the army and the navy felt that the zeppelin was outliving its usefulness and that enemy bases and cities could be more effectively attacked by airplanes armored and equipped as bombers. By the end of the summer of 1917, formations of twin-engined Gothas and four-engine Giants were being launched on a succession of raids over the heart of London, not only at night but also in daring strikes during daylight. Their success was questionable in terms of damage inflicted on the British, but their supporters dealt a blow to the zeppelin program by forcing cutbacks in aluminum and other strategic supplies for airships and increasing such allotments for the bombers. Strasser found himself forced to restrict his raids over England to times when the nights were unusually dark and at altitudes where he knew that his ships could not be struck either by antiaircraft fire or by incendiary bullets from small, high-flying planes.

Many commanders would have given in to the inevitable and taken these setbacks in stride as one of the bad fortunes of war.

But not Strasser. He was more determined than ever now to push his men and ships to levels never before imagined. He knew that he could count on the officers and men of the Naval Airship Division because his engineers had overcome some of the altitude problems that had plagued earlier flights. Moreover, morale in the division was high, his fleet was strong and not plagued by recent losses, and the British were disheartened by their inability to lay so much as a finger on zeppelins coming in at eighteen thousand feet or higher. If he could orchestrate one more massive, record-breaking attack on London, the high command would waver in its loyalties. And at that point he would plunge in and demand a vast increase in the zeppelin program—something that would aim a staggering blow at England and quickly shorten the war.

Thus it was that he planned what later was to become known as the Silent Raid.

THE GREAT ZEPPELIN GAMBLE

T

he officers of the Naval Airship Division were riding high in more ways than one in the early fall of 1917. They had all but conquered the physiological and psychological problems of commanding zeppelins at extremely high altitudes. During the course of an intensive training program mechanics and flight engineers had devised methods of keeping their engines humming steadily in extremes of cold. And the men had been trained effectively in ways to breathe properly through the still-primitive but slightly improved oxygen masks and avoid altitude sickness and disabling physical ailments.

Secretly, word was making the rounds that Strasser was planning a mission that would rank as one of the major raids of the war. From the highest commander to the lowest enlisted man this was great news. Everyone was tired of hearing about the exploits of the Gothas and Giants and U-boats. It was time for zeppelins to get back into the action.

Bets were placed as to the raid's date; those who pinpointed 19 October on their calendars were the winners.

By this time there were six new ships of the L-50 class in operation. They were 644 feet long and 92 feet high, held a volume of almost two million cubic feet of gas, and could lift almost 90,000 pounds, including men, equipment, fuel, ballast, ammunition, and more than three tons of bombs. They were powered by five Maybach HSL engines with a combined rating of more than 1,200 horsepower.

The name *Silent Raid* was applied to the mission when it was announced that the airships would fly at such a high altitude that the sound of their engines could not be heard on the ground except through orthophones or other mechanical or radio devices. Although London was initially selected as the target, plans were modified to bring about "a rain of destruction" on industrial centers in the Midlands, which were producing planes, munitions, and other strategic war supplies. The Germans were hopeful that they could prove the deadly accuracy and effectiveness of a new bombsight that had been perfected for high-altitude bombing. It made use of radio waves beamed toward the ground that provided a pattern to show more accurately than previous methods the airship's ground speed and direction. Bombardiers could thus determine when to release their bombs so they would arc toward the intended target as the zeppelin approached and proceeded over it.

The air was cold and leaden as dawn broke over the dark zeppelin sheds at Tondern. Outside, the scene was deceptively quiet as German sentries paced their rounds, occasionally pulling their topcoats tighter around the neck to shut out the mists swirling down from the North Sea some fifty miles away. Inside the dual shed, however, there was intense activity around the two great black-bellied zeppelins housed together, *L-45* and *L-54*.

In the small operations shack Kapitänleutnant Waldemar Kolle of the *L-45* paced the dusty floor and glanced repeatedly at his watch. "Won't that damned Tree Frog ever call in?" he muttered to the other airship commander present, Oberleutnant Bockholt von Buttlar, skipper of the *L-54*.

"Give him time. Give him time," muttered Buttlar sleepily. Tree Frog was the code name for the meteorologist whose weather report would be the deciding factor in the launching of a raid. "Besides, we'll be getting our instructions direct from Strasser himself when he arrives."

"Strasser!" Kolle stopped pacing abruptly. "He's coming over from Nordholz?"

"Yes. *L-54* has a passenger this trip." Buttlar was a long-faced wry little man but one of the most experienced and capable Luftschiffe officers in the naval service. "He'll probably expect me to do everything but fly under London Bridge!"

Kolle strode out of the shack without further words and collared his adjutant to inform him that the Chief was soon to arrive and that *L-45* had damned well better be in perfect trim. Strasser was a strict perfectionist. The slightest oversight in the handling of an airship could evoke from him a scowl and a clipped word of rebuke that would make even the most hardened flight officer break out in a cold sweat.

"Check out all engines at once," he ordered his flight engineer.

Soon the zeppelin shed was bedlam as one engine after another coughed into motion amid shouts of "Contact!" . . . "Mind the propellers!" . . . "Clutch in!" Somehow the roar was comforting to Kolle as he glanced intently along every section of the 643 feet of thin black fabric that encased the airship.

Kolle did not reflect on the sight long. There was too much to do. He walked out of the great shed into the comparative stillness of the dawn. He did not like the feel of the weather. It was too close and heavy, as though some kind of pressure were squeezing down from the north. Well, the strategic evaluation of the weather—that was up to Tree Frog and Strasser. Kolle checked out the handling parties, the men who would soon load ammunition and bombs from the underground dumps, who would hose in water for the ballast tanks, and who would have the ticklish job of easing the zeppelin out of the shed during those critical moments before she could be controlled by engine power.

For the next two hours the sound of engines rose and fell, gradually easing from the staccato wheezing of cold pistons to the steady purr of mechanical readiness as each Maybach was warmed up, checked out, and then thrown into idle. Now the last bombs had been slung on their racks; the ammunition belts had been carefully fed into the machine guns; and the hydrogen gas valves had been cautiously bled to check for leaks and sluggishness. Now, too, the water ballast tanks were full; the long hoses were slowly being reeled out of the keel housing; and the sandbags tied to the handling rails along the gondolas fore and aft were being loosened for quick maneuvering.

At ten-thirty on that October morning Kolle saw his young adjutant approaching on the double. "*He's* here, Sir," said the officer briskly.

Kolle returned quickly to the operations shack and smartly saluted the wiry little man who stood before him. Strasser returned the salute. He gave no other greeting. He did not smile. He was all business as usual when a raid was getting under way— quite the opposite of what he could be on a relaxed evening in the officers' mess or in one of the local bars frequented by officers of the Naval Airship Division. The Führer der Luftschiffe seemed intense and cold-eyed to many, with a smallish head that always made his Imperial Navy cap seem too large for him. Beneath the piercing dark eyes and the strong nose, his features were distinguished by a carefully trimmed mustache and a thin goatee. He wore a high white collar that contrasted sharply with the dark blue of his naval uniform, and beneath the collar hung the Iron Cross he had been awarded by the Kaiser and which he had earned many times over during raids on England.

Fregatenkapitän Peter Strasser was the only man in all Germany who could have walked the taut high wire that symbolized his position as head of the zeppelin forces. A slip in any direction meant death, for his own personal, dedicated interpretation of leadership dictated that he had to make as many of the treacherous raids on England as he required his officers to do in any given period. He was sometimes called a man obsessed. Yet his own evaluation was that he was simply doing his duty. And there was never any doubt that he had won the admiration and respect of his superior, Admiral Reinhard Scheer, in command of the German fleet.

"You will take *L-45* out of the shed first, Commander," he said finally, as Kolle stood at attention. "Then *L-54* will follow. I don't have to warn you that we have some tricky crosswinds."

"We are ready, Sir," replied Kolle crisply, "and I have already instructed the handlers to keep a heavy hand on the ship until we are free and clear."

"We ascend at twelve noon. Sharp." He paused thoughtfully. "It will be middle England tonight, as you already know." That meant the big industrial centers that belted England at the waist—Hull, York, Leeds, Sheffield, Manchester. "Further weather reports will be transmitted as soon as we hear from Tree

Frog again. Good luck!" Peter Strasser turned on one heel and walked out to inspect *L-54*.

Once again the great shed at Tondern was alive with action. The shed captain had the doors open on the end away from the wind. The handling party was posted at the ropes and along the gondola rails of *L-45* and *L-54*. Kolle swung himself up into the control car forward.

"All clear for leaving the shed!" shouted the officer of the watch from a vantage point at the open doors where he could keep an eye on both the ship and the wind sock outside. Kolle gave a curt wave with one gloved hand, standing erect at the celluloid-encased bow. A shrill whistle came from his engine officer in the gondola aft.

"Airship *Ma-a-a-a-rch*!" sang out the ground sergeant.

Slowly the huge airship eased out of the shed. The wind tugged at her nose the instant it poked through the open doors, but the ground crew was ready and the ship was held straight.

About three hundred yards out of the shed the idling motors were clutched in. Propellers in *L-45*'s five 210-horsepower engines began to spin slowly. At the same instant the ground crew deftly unreeved all trailing lines and gripped the huge black monster by the rails running fore and aft along each of the two main gondolas.

"Stand by for ascent!" ordered Kolle, quickly following the command with "Up one!" The bow gondola was instantly released by the ground crew and the great blunt nose began to rise into the somber sky.

"Up two!" The stern car was released and the entire ship became airborne. Within minutes she had floated skyward to a thousand feet, still using her engines minimally to maintain position and balance while all controls and equipment were given a final inspection and operational check.

Ten minutes later power was ordered and *L-45* picked up enough speed so that her forward motion, stabilized by the giant tail fins, planed her through the mists at a speed of forty knots.

Kolle glanced at his watch. It was seven minutes past noon. Behind and below he could see *L-54* moving out of the shed steadily. He knew that Strasser would be aboard that ship, one of the largest and newest in the German airship fleet. "Due north by northwest," he ordered the navigator. "Our first bearing is Helgoland."

Meanwhile, in similar sheds in Nordholz and Oldenburg to the north, the same scenes were being reenacted as thirteen giant zeppelins prepared for the greatest mass raid yet undertaken. It was not the largest in terms of sheer numbers (sixteen had been dispatched on one previous raid), but it was by far the most ambitious in terms of total bomb load and firepower and the mission's objectives.

Strategically, it was the most significant because all of the ships were of the "super" type and because Strasser now had his back against the wall in his attempts to prove once and for all that the zeppelin—even more than the U-boat—represented Germany's one proud hope of beating the Allies into submission.

Kolle knew that Strasser had been on some of the very earliest airship raids in the primitive *L-5*, *L-6*, and *L-7*, fragile, lumbering craft that had earned the zeppelin the once scornful title "the balloon with a paddle." He had originated the steady shuttle route from Germany across the North Sea to the mouth of the Humber in the later *L-10*, *L-11*, and *L-12*. He had led the nine-ship mass raid on the Midlands back in January 1916. And he had watched so many airships go down in flames nearby while his own ship miraculously escaped enemy antiaircraft fire and attack planes that it was said he could no longer watch when a sister ship was hit but would cover his face with his hands and remain unable to speak.

It would have crushed almost any commander to realize, as Strasser did, that the casualty rate for his officers and men—killed, wounded, or captured—had climbed to 40 percent. And that, statistically, fate marked two out of every five zeppelins to crash in flames in combat or be destroyed by accident in their sheds. How many military leaders in all of history, Kolle wondered, had been called upon to face such odds? He could think of none. Yet Strasser not only persisted in his single-minded aim but continually convinced his subordinates that victory was truly within their grasp.

By twelve-thirty that October afternoon, the dark, deadly giants were in the air and headed for their rendezvous, scheduled for the English coast just after dusk. It was not learned until eleven of the ships were airborne and gliding silently across the North Sea at an altitude of thirteen thousand feet that two ships of the intended armada—*L-42* and *L-51*—were never to leave their hangars because of vicious crosswinds. So the fleet was composed of eleven ships instead of thirteen, by numbers *L-41*, *L-44*, *L-45*, *L-46*, *L-47*, *L-49*, *L-50*, *L-52*, *L-53*, *L-54*, and *L-55*. Each crew consisted of the commander, his first officer, two petty officers (navigator and bombardier), a chief engineman, six mechanics, a sailmaker (responsible for repairing the envelope, gasbags, and other fabrics), an electrician, and ten other ranks who handled height and directional wheels, machine guns, and various flight instruments.

During a bomb run the commander traditionally operated "the bomb-aimer's switchboard" with the help of the bombardier, deciding which missiles to release, and in what order, in a payload that ranged widely: from incendiaries to 25-pounders, 110-pounders, and in some cases a lone 650-pound blockbuster. During the bomb runs, the navigator had the trickiest assignment of all, trying to hold the ship directly over the target despite wind, cranky engines, searchlight glare, antiaircraft fire, and other disconcerting factors.

In the event of attack by fighter planes, several of the mechanics were usually allocated to man the machine guns with the regular gunners. Since the zeppelin service was an elite corps formed of hand-picked men who had to exhibit numerous skills, most crew members were well trained to perform three or four specialized duties with equal facility. Whatever the criticisms leveled against the Luftschiffe by the enemy and German political opponents alike, there can be no question that the courage and dedication of airshipmen was of the highest order. And if some were said to carry small vials of poison for quick death if their ships were shot down in flames, it can be countered that even the bravest have some limits of endurance.

Aboard *L-45* as she headed for the Helgoland bearing point westward across the North Sea, Kapitänleutnant Waldemar Kolle nursed his ship gradually up to thirteen thousand feet, Strasser's prearranged cruising altitude. During the rise in elevation from ten thousand to thirteen thousand, however, he had noticed a distinct change in the ship's performance. He did not like it.

"The wind is increasing," reported the navigator. "It was fifteen knots northwest. Now I make it thirty knots, and swinging more from the north."

Kolle nodded but remained silent as the ship continued into a darkening sky. Through his sighting periscope he could make out the dark shapes of several other airships and assumed that *L-54*, with Strasser aboard in his usual role of observer, was in the lead position.

"Land ahead!" Just before 6:00 P.M., the lookout atop the bag informed the commander by intercom phone that they had reached their landfall.

"Up bow. Rudders steady. Engines full. Ascend to sixteen

thousand feet." Kolle gave the order that he judged would be given by all of the other airship commanders to put them safely out of range of antiaircraft fire. There could be no doubt that the British must be on the alert. They had greatly improved their coastal observation system and the acoustical and wireless equipment used to detect approaching airships and bombers.

As *L-45* climbed it was evident to even the most inexperienced enlisted man aboard that she was headed for trouble. The upper atmosphere was turbulent with crosswinds—the kind that could rip tail fins, smash gondola windscreens, and even twist the fragile skeleton of the ship itself.

On 19 October 1917 Great Britain lay between a center of high pressure located over the Bay of Biscay in southwestern France and low pressure over Iceland to the northwest of Scotland. From the ground up to an elevation of about ten thousand feet over the English Midlands the air was still, held in a strange vacuum. At an altitude above twenty thousand feet, however, a raging gale was swinging down from the northwest. In the layer in between (from ten thousand to twenty thousand feet, where the zeppelins were flying) the air was unstable and ominously turbulent. Headwinds would prevent most of the airships from reaching their intended objectives that night. Already, crosscurrents were warping the 650-foot hulls so that the fabric could be seen rippling and the framework could be heard groaning and shuddering. Fitful gusts tore at the tail fins so severely that it was difficult for the ruddermen to hold any kind of steady course, much less hope to home in on targets below.

It was ironic that the persevering, ultrameticulous Peter Strasser, who had endured months of agonizing patience to coordinate his forces and wait for the propitious moment to strike, should be caught up in this turn of events that left him at the mercy of wind and weather. It was even more ironic that Strasser was not to realize what tragedy was in the making until long after the fateful course of events had reached a point of no return.

By 11:00 P.M. northern England was being swept by winds of gale force, with gusts up to sixty knots. In London to the south, however, the air was strangely calm. Lieutenant Colonel A. M. Rawlinson of the British Home Guard had received a report from his east-coast observation posts that "ten or more" German zeppelins had crossed the North Sea. For the next few hours he was to become perhaps the most confused and frustrated officer in all of England.

"If ten zeppelins have sneaked in," he bellowed at his communications officer, where in bloody hell are they?"

The officer, a shaggy and inexperienced young lieutenant who had hoped to be fighting the Huns face-to-face in France and not assigned to the "geriatric corps," shook his blond head with a perplexed look. As he tried vainly to explain, three listening posts equipped with orthophones had reported the approach of unidentified aircraft. Then, as quickly as these ears had picked up the sounds of distant engines they had lost them again. During the next hour the exasperation of the Home Guard officers became more pronounced than ever when several observation posts in the Midlands reported exploding bombs in their zones but no sounds of aircraft engines at all.

"My God!" gasped Rawlinson at 10:00 P.M., his face beaded with sweat. "We're being given a new kind of treatment by those Boche bastards—a *silent raid!*"

Dismissing the lieutenant's suggestion that maybe a raiding party with dynamite charges had landed in small boats, the colonel came up with his own deduction: The Germans had flown upwind of their targets, turned their engines off to avoid detection, and were drifting downwind like balloons and dropping bombs whenever they passed over a likely target.

"In such a case," he explained, "the orthophones and wireless detectors would pick up no sounds. And our ground observers and searchlights couldn't penetrate the cloud layers above which the airships are moving."

The sounds of explosives and the inability to see or hear the enemy brought a new kind of terror to the British in the cities of the Midlands that night. Now all of the rumors about superzeppelins with deadly accurate bombsights and huge bombs swept the civilian population with cold fear. Warnings of a possible invasion by a cloudborne army sprouted on all sides. And the shaken population did not know whether to flee to the country, where they might encounter invading troops blockading the roads, or cower in city cellars where they might be at the mercy of the bombs.

"Phone instructions to all observation and command posts," ordered Rawlinson as the commanders of the Home Guard units tried to keep their heads, "to keep searchlights off." In the pitch-darkness of this particularly dark night, he reasoned, zeppelin commanders would surely lose their bearings.

What the British did not realize until much later was that the Silent Raid was caused by factors other than shutting off the engines. High altitude played a part, of course. But even more, the freak winds completely blotted out the roar of engines despite the fact that most were racing at full speed in order to maintain maneuverability. The freak nature of the storm was such that down on the ground the sound of exploding bombs might be heard fifty miles away and yet not be heard at all in the upwind parts of the cities in which they were falling.

At a few minutes past ten that evening, air-raid alarms shrieked their raucous warnings through the heart of London. The inhabitants raced to their inadequate bomb shelters—cellars for the most part, or makeshift "igloos" constructed with sandbags and rusting sheet metal. Above them, in the blackness, they pictured a huge armada of lethal cigar-shaped dragons, each one capable of wiping out an entire city block with a single one of their bombs.

The British were not the only ones in confusion. When Kapitänleutnant Waldemar Kolle brought *L-45* in over the Yorkshire coast at 8:50 P.M. he was already having almost insurmountable problems. The Maybach engines, developed in the days when ten-thousand-foot altitude was high for an airship, had been modified to endure long periods of cold. But even these fine performers began to balk at the lack of oxygen and plummeting temperature associated with increasing altitudes. As Kolle rose to eighteen thousand feet the crankshafts began to squeal and the exhausts to wheeze as the propellers clawed at the wind and thin air. When he risked bringing the airship down to fourteen thousand feet he was unprepared when he was suddenly jumped by a British night fighter that had somehow managed to spot the dark airship against a bank of clouds. He was astounded that a plane could have ventured into the air at all in such wild turbulence.

"Here she comes! Directly below!"

The attacker was a Sopwith Camel of a type specially adapted for attacking in the dark and was, Kolle knew full well, easily capable of downing an airship by raking it with incendiary bullets from its Lewis gun. Kolle took immediate evasive action, ordering ballast dropped and the huge stern elevators tilted so the bow would angle upward and the ship would climb fast. In the darkness, he and his observers would have difficulty keeping track of the attacker except when he was unleashing a round of incendiaries. And by then it might be too late. His only escape route was upward—as fast as possible.

"Drop more ballast!" Kolle shouted to the chief engineer. They would not be safe until they reached nineteen thousand feet at least.

Just as he thought they would make it, he heard the chatter of machine-gun fire from astern and saw tracers arcing toward the lower fin. Then, inexplicably, the sound vanished and there was no more evidence of the Sopwith. As it turned out later, the pilot, a Lieutenant Harrison of the Royal Flying Corps, based at the Stanford Aerodrome, had jammed his gun just at the moment he was zeroing in for the kill.

At 10:50 P.M., mistaking some ground lights for a factory at Oxford, Kolle dropped five 110-pounders and nine incendiaries before realizing his error. Shortly afterward, his observer spotted what looked like a railway line headed in the same direction *L-45* was being pushed by the increasing winds.

"I think we're running straight for London," he reported to the commander.

Kolle hunched over the chart table, risking the use of a shielded lamp for a few seconds. He decided the observer was correct. London had not been listed as an objective for any of the airships that night. But if fortune were going to force his hand, he was willing to play the cards accordingly.

By eleven-fifteen *L-45* had reached the northwestern corner of the city. She was making well over sixty knots going southeasterly with the wind. So strong was the gale now that the helmsman could not have changed course more than a few degrees, and even then only at the risk of putting a dangerous strain on the ship's hull and framework. Zeppelins had been known to break in half under such wind pressure. After all, the ship was almost as long as the ill-fated liner *Lusitania* and could hardly sustain a wall of wind thudding against the envelope for very long.

Perhaps the most remarkable aspect of this bombing run was that, although the bombardier was barely able to sight much of the city through the clouds, all the remaining bombs in *L-45*'s racks hit strategic points in London. The first strikes were at Hendon, near the airfield. The next struck railway sidings at Cricklewood. And several plunged directly into the heart of the city near Piccadilly Circus.

On the ground, there was consternation and disagreement at Home Guard headquarters. Some officers were in favor of activating the searchlights and trying to catch the raider through a break in the clouds. Others argued that the zeppelin was too high to reach with either antiaircraft barrages or fighter planes and hence any light on the ground would aid the Hun. In any case, the attack was over before they reached a decision, leaving a death toll of thirty-six and almost sixty wounded. The amount of damage was questionable—and in terms of World War II bombings laughable. But the psychological trauma was great, especially since the British had been so exultant about recent zeppelin losses and the success of the fighter planes in the nighttime David-and-Goliath battles.

The intense fear of mass raids was so great that it even stimulated articles in newspapers in the United States; a typical one carried the headline, Can the Germans Bomb New York by Air?

After the last bomb was dropped, the *L-45*'s moment of glory was turned into a desperate battle to survive. The gale drove her southward across the English Channel. Kolle tried to beat his way eastward toward German soil. It was no use. He jettisoned his last drop of water and other expendables in an attempt to rise above the winds. The cries of "Oxygen!" rang out as the ship bucked and yawed her way up to twenty thousand feet and the men used the tubes and mouthpieces of a new breathing device that had been invented for high-altitude flight. But this new equipment was far from perfect and, as a result, some of the men vomited or started bleeding from the nose, ears, and mouth. A few lapsed into unconsciousness.

The altitude combined with the subzero temperature was now threatening the engines as well. One went dead, its cooling system frozen. The others, which could not produce more than 50 percent power at that height under the best of circumstances, began missing and were also in imminent danger of going dead.

Altitude proved to be no solution to the storm in any case. By three in the morning Kolle knew he had lost the last round as *L-45* careened drunkenly over the French coast and was swept southward toward Amiens. Dawn found her some forty miles east of Paris, deep in the heart of enemy territory.

"The best we can do is try to reach Switzerland," he told his navigator after studying the charts. Speaking on behalf of the crew as well as himself, he knew it would be far better to be interned in neutral territory than to be captured by the French.

Just after dawn, there was a moment of excitement when one of the lookouts shouted "Airships! Airships!"

Everyone who heard the cry immediately froze, certain that this was a warning that fighter planes were attacking. But then Kolle saw them—two other zeppelins far to the east and almost invisible in the haze. These were *L-49* and *L-50*, soon to be joined by *L-44*. Gazing at them from afar and glancing earthward through breaks in the clouds at enemy territory far below, Kolle did not have to stretch his imagination to see a multiple tragedy in the making.

While the four zeppelins over France were using every alternative in the book to try to escape their fate, other airships in the armada were faring somewhat better. By remarkable skill and good fortune, seven of the original eleven managed to weather the gale and return to German-held territory, if not to their own bases, during that fateful Saturday morning, 20 October. In *L-54* Buttlar had already circled back over the North Sea after dropping his full bomb load on what he had made out to be industrial targets in Derby and Nottingham. His high-ranking passenger, Peter Strasser, expressed high praise for the performance of the officers and crew and hazarded a guess that the mass raid had been a huge success despite the stormy weather.

"The High Command will have to listen to us now," he said confidently as L-54 eased her way gracefully down toward the air base at Tondern while dawn was breaking. "If we can shuttle almost forty tons of bombs over military objectives in the midst of a raging storm, imagine what our new ships can do under more favorable conditions." His eyes glinted and Buttlar did not know when he had seen his superior so jubilant in recent months.

The first reports bore him out. L-46 had made runs over Walcott, dropping ten high-explosive bombs. Then she unloaded the rest on factories near Ruston in the Midlands. Her skipper, Kapitänleutnant Heinrich Hollender, was certain he had caused "immense damage to industrial facilities." L-47 had dropped bombs on Wittering Aerodrome, Holbeach, and Spalding near The Wash on the east coast of England before returning to Germany over The Netherlands, a route taken also by L-54 and L-46.

L-41 reported even more success. Hauptmann Kumo Manger had hit the large city of Birmingham, in the very heart of England. After that he had pressed his luck to the north and had the good fortune to spot the Austin Motor Works at Longridge, which had its night-shift lights on, never expecting an attack that far inland and distant from London. At least one high-explosive bomb registered a direct hit.

L-52 had more difficulty with the weather but had been able to hit the southeastern region of England, where she struck targets at Kemsworth, Hertford, and Waltham. She had experienced moments of excitement when chased by a British fighter plane but had easily been able to rise quickly above the plane's ceiling and avoid its attack.

"That bears me out," Strasser had said, putting down the

phone after *L-52*'s report had come in. "Our new ships can stay beyond the reach of the enemy. We have just had word, too, from *L-53*, that she avoided attack planes in the same way and dropped some unwelcome presents on our British friends."

There was only one sour note that morning. *L-55*, which had bombed the Great Northern Railway and nearby installations, had been forced too far south by the gale-force winds and had found herself directly over the Western Front. After being dogged by (but avoiding) several Allied planes and almost running out of fuel, she had been damaged heavily in a crash landing in central Germany. In the course of this action, however, she had accomplished an amazing feat. To avoid the planes and the artillery fire he could see below him all along the front, her commander, Hans Kurt Flemming, had taken the ship up to the unprecedented height of twenty-four thousand feet.*

As Strasser passed along initial reports to the naval high command and retired to the officers' club with a mug of coffee to await similar word from the other zeppelin commanders, he did not know that the whole tragedy would be coming to a bitter climax that morning.

As Kapitänleutnant Waldeman Kolle watched *L-49*, *L-50*, and later *L-44* in the distance, he began to realize with horror that something was disastrously wrong. The three ships were now in what looked like a definite formation led by *L-44*, whose captain seemed to know just where he was heading. Even at the distance that separated them from Kolle's high-flying *L-45*, he estimated that all three were cruising at an altitude of not more than five thousand feet.

"Good God," he rasped hoarsely to his navigator. "They have

---

* This was a record never surpassed even by the big dirigibles of the 1920s and 1930s.

veered so far off course they don't realize they are over *French* soil and think they are now in Germany!"

He ordered his wireless operator to break silence and try to get through to them at all costs. The wireless crackled away in its relentless warning to no avail. Either the ships had their wireless stations closed down or there was a problem with transmission.

During this desperate action the officers and men aboard *L-45* could see puffs of black in the sky as a French antiaircraft battery opened up on the zeppelin trio. One of the ships (it turned out to be *L-44*) immediately started an abrupt change of course and tilted her bow skyward. It was obvious that full speed had been ordered and she was trying to climb beyond antiaircraft range. But it was too late. A shell pierced one of the hydrogen bags aft. Through his glasses Kolle saw a thin red line rise up the side as though made by a giant paint brush. Then the whole stern burst into a mass of flame. Within seconds the airship was nothing but a fiery form in the sky. She faltered, then broke sickeningly in two and plummeted to earth.

L-49 and *L-50*, suddenly aware of their own danger, climbed skyward as fast as they could. But tragedy was closing in. Before he could gain enough altitude to climb out of range, Kapitän Hans Gayer of *L-49* saw himself looking into the jaws of death again, this time in the guise of Escadrille 152, a flight of five Nieuport planes under the command of a determined flight lieutenant named Lefevre. As it turned out, Lefevre was not at all intent on making a flaming coffin for the Huns but had set his sights on capturing a classic prize. Whenever the *L-49* tried to rise, he and his four other fighters came in with guns blazing tracers—but always aimed just above the top of the zeppelin.

In the end Gayer, much shaken by the sight of *L-44* afire barely half an hour earlier, saw that escape was impossible. If he pushed the issue until the French were low on fuel, they would indubitably elect to shoot him down before heading back to their base. He ordered *L-49* down, destroying all of her documents before settling to a field where he purposely landed more heavily than necessary in order to damage the ship as much as possible. As he could clearly see, three of the Nieuport fighter pilots were landing ahead of him and would be at the zeppelin's side before the crew could destroy the airship.

Thus it was that *L-49* became one of World War I's most valued prizes. (Later, copied seam for seam and rib for rib, she became the prototype for the United States navy dirigible *Shenandoah*.)

L-50 might have escaped the Allies except for a curious blunder. Her skipper, Kapitänleutnant Roderick Schwonder, piloted his ship southward that morning as the storm diminished. For a while he was alone in the clouds, circling and trying with great difficulty to establish reliable bearings. Then, through a break in the cloud cover, he sighted an airship on the ground. "We have reached a German base," he called excitedly, knowing that the craft could only be one of his sister ships. Because of navigational problems, he had no idea that he was really near Dommartin, a French village near the German border.

He ordered *L-50* down to within five hundred feet of the ground and only then did he realize with astonishment that the ship was *L-49* and the men surrounding her French troops. In their haste to rise out of range as they were assaulted by a barrage of rifle fire, the crewmen mishandled the controls. The nose went up in an emergency climb position, which caused the tail to dip so low that it smashed into a stand of tall trees, making the whole ship fishtail and roll. Within less than a minute the gondolas had been ripped off by the forward motion as they lurched against other trees.

Some of the German officers and men were trapped in the

wreckage of the gondolas until they could force their way to freedom. Others tumbled out onto the soft ground, relatively unhurt. But four crew members who were inside the keel section or on the topside machine-gun post were swept aloft when the now-lightened hull rose again into the sky. Later, far in the south of France, the hull of *L-50* was sighted high in the sky, dangling its snapped cables and wallowing crazily as it headed still farther southward toward the Mediterranean. Neither ship nor men were ever seen again.

That left only the *L-45* to be accounted for.

Commander Kolle managed to evade artillery fire and enemy fighter planes partly because he was farther from the front lines and the trenches than any of the other ships and partly because he was able to reach protective cloud cover. But the engines in the forward and port cars and one in the stern gondola had broken down completely, leaving him with only two that were operable. For several hours he tried to beat his way northeast toward Geneva, Switzerland. Internment in neutral territory was certainly preferable to capture by the French, who held a violent hatred of the Germans because of U-boat sinkings and reported atrocities, even though they had been spared zeppelin raids on their cities.

By 10:30 A.M., almost out of fuel, with little power left in his remaining engines, and with the entire crew near mental and physical exhaustion, Kolle made his decision. "All hands prepare for landing." He did not know exactly where he was, but the terrain below seemed to be open countryside, rural, and devoid of military installations or activity. With luck some of the men might make an escape on foot or steal a boat and go down a winding river they had spotted below.

Kolle had just enough of an idea of his bearings to realize that if they remained in the air much longer they would soon be out over the Mediterranean, where they might easily be blasted out of the sky by naval batteries. He selected the almost-dry stony bed of what he later learned was a tributary of the Durance River near the town of Sisteron in Provence. It was the only location clear of trees he could see and there were no people in sight. He ordered the maneuvering valves of the ship opened and the two emergency pennants displayed so that enemy observers—if indeed there were any in the vicinity—could see that the ship was in trouble and would not be trying to escape.

"Captain, we are losing control!" the helmsman shouted above the wheezing of the remaining engines, discovering that the wheel would not respond effectively against the turbulent air currents in the valley. Kolle sprang to the wheel to give him a hand, but the control surfaces of the tail fins failed to respond.

"Open valves full!" he commanded. "All hands be fully prepared. We are going down *hard*!"

The control gondola crunched into the river bed. As it did a gust caught the great hull above and heeled the zeppelin on her side. The tail warped around more than ninety degrees. As hydrogen gas hissed out of the emergency valves, *L-45* slumped down in one piece and the officers and men scrambled free of the wreckage with only minor cuts and bruises.

Kolle ordered his men to form ranks a hundred feet from the downed airship. Then he methodically collected all of their personal identification. This he placed with the ship's charts and documents in the partially crumpled control car. The navigator then fired the ship with incendiary flares. The crew stood at attention in the heat and glare as *L-45* went up in smoke. It was 10:45 A.M.

Minutes later Kolle was surprised to see that a man who came running from a clump of trees was an infantry sergeant major in a German uniform. His initial impression was that he had made an astonishing error regarding his bearings and was really in his homeland. But his hope was dashed when the sergeant explained that he was in charge of a work party of German prisoners from a nearby military internment camp.

"There is little chance that any of you can escape," the sergeant explained apologetically. "Because of the prison camp, this whole area is well patrolled by guards, dogs, and electrical detectors. I advise you to come with me to the French commandant and surrender. He is quite a tolerant person and, besides, the camp here at Sisteron is better than most others you might be confined to."

Thus ended the war for Kapitänleutnant Waldemar Kolle and his crew, less tragically than it had for many of the best men in the elite zeppelin service.

CHAPTER 11

TO THE BITTER END

All morning long after his return to Tondern on *L-54* on Saturday 20 October, Peter Strasser had sat in the small mess room of the officers' club awaiting reports and in general exulting over what he referred to as the "historic success" of the great zeppelin raid. He was positive that his eleven ships had succeeded in bringing more destruction to military targets in England than any previous raid. And he was even more buoyed by the fact that his new 40 and 50 classes of zeppelin could hit targets with more accuracy than ever and yet remain well out of range of antiaircraft barrages and night fighters. With a new type of bombsight now being perfected, it could logically be expected that future raids would be deadlier than ever. Furthermore, there was no chance whatsoever that British technology could develop antiaircraft guns that would range higher or aircraft that could attain much greater altitudes than was now possible. The Germans surely had an enviable military advantage.

Although Strasser's optimism about the fate of the other ships in the armada grew weaker with each passing hour, not until afternoon did the first disquieting news come to him.

"We have just heard," reported one of the adjutants in the headquarters office of the Naval Airship Division, "that a zeppelin was shot down over France somewhere near St. Clement in the Lorraine region."

Strasser, who by this time had pored over the log books of the airships that had already reported in, waved his right hand impatiently. "Impossible!" he grunted with a look of disbelief. "What would a German airship be doing that far south, almost to Switzerland?"

"We don't know yet, Sir. But we're trying to get a reliable report." The adjutant was as shaken by his superior's reaction as by the possibility of the loss itself.

Then, late that afternoon, Strasser received an urgent call to appear at headquarters. When he arrived he knew instantly that the news was not good. "We have just received intelligence reports," said a grim-faced admiral, "that have enough specific details to confirm our fears that L-44 was shot down in flames, L-45 crash-landed in enemy territory and had to be destroyed by her own crew, and L-50 is missing in southern France—almost as far south as the Mediterranean."

He held out a decoded message. "That is not all," said the admiral. "We have just received word that L-49 was forced down by fighter planes and . . ."

163

"Shot down?" interrupted Strasser.

"Not shot down, but forced down—and *captured*!"

The zeppelin commander's face turned deathly white. Captured? That was impossible. He had given explicit orders that an airship must never be taken intact. And to assure that this would always be so, he had trained each crew relentlessly and tirelessly in methods of instant destruction should a ship ever be forced down on enemy soil. It was even better to go down in flames than to suffer this greatest disgrace of all.

In the end, Strasser had to accept the fact that with four out of eleven ships lost and a fifth seriously damaged in a crash landing, and with nearly a hundred officers and men killed or captured, no amount of damage inflicted on the British could have compensated for the loss to Germany. Yet he did not flinch in his efforts to convince his superiors in the navy that the zeppelin was still the weapon that would ultimately break England's back. His arguments were forceful enough to retain the support of Admiral Scheer, and he was able to extract a promise from the Admiralty that it would underwrite the cost of a new breed of super-superzeppelins he had requested, some twenty ships to be numbered in the L-60s and L-70s.

No matter how critical historians may be of the Naval Airship Division and the place of the zeppelin in the course of World War I, it must be remembered that the invention of airships as a strategic weapon was unequaled in military history at the time— even surpassing the development of the submarine. (A more modern counterpart as a weapon to terrorize an enemy homeland might be the liquid-fueled V-2 rocket the Germans invented and used as a ballistic missile against London late in World War II.)

Another astonishing fact of zeppelin warfare was that, when Peter Strasser was assigned the impossible task of molding and directing a brand-new arm of the service, he had never been in an airship, had no technical knowledge of lighter-than-air craft, and had been neither tutored nor trained in combat strategy. According to Captain Hans von Schiller, Strasser was nothing short of a genius.

"With tremendous energy, Strasser studied all aspects of his new field and only now did his real abilities show themselves," Schiller explained much later. "He was an organizer, firm of purpose, who recognized and developed the still-unsuspected possibilities of the airship for scouting and as a weapon of offense. When the war broke out, the Naval Airship Division had only the *L-3* at its disposal, and Peter Strasser set out with the full force of his strong personality to promote the development of this new weapon.

"In a very few months, airship ports were created on the North Sea and Baltic coasts and airships were stationed there. By 1916, the Naval Airship Division had grown from 120 to nearly 7,000 officers and men, distributed over twelve naval airports. As many as twenty-five ships were in service simultaneously. By the end of 1916, Strasser was appointed Commander-in-Chief of the naval airships and six months later he received the *Pour le Merite*, the highest military distinction."

As Schiller (who knew Strasser well) emphasized, Strasser never once flinched, not even when five of his newest ships were annihilated at Ahlhorn within thirty seconds, whether by accident or sabotage no one will ever know. Most important, he continued relentlessly to press for technical and engineering design improvements so that the once-flimsy and slow-moving airship became a superzeppelin in the short span of little more than three years. It is unnerving to think what the zeppelin might have been had Germany had access to supplies of helium or other gases that were safer and more stable than hydrogen.

In many ways, while the zeppelin failed to win the war, its

accomplishments were often impressive. The long, much-disputed mission of the *L-59* is a case in point.

In the late summer of 1917 it was evident to the German high command that it was fighting a losing battle against the British in the Makonde Highlands of German East Africa. General Paul von Lettow-Vorbeck had for many months been waging what was referred to, with great understatement, as a rear-guard action to try to hold the last German outpost in an area that is now part of Tanzania. All attempts to send badly needed supplies to him had met with failure.

Now it was suggested that a zeppelin, stripped of all possible accessories and, of course, carrying no bomb load, could carry as many as fifteen tons of supplies in a single trip. After a little pressure from the army and the colonial office, the navy agreed to assign the new *L-59* to the project. This ship was, in reality, the *L-57* lengthened and provided with additional hydrogen gas cells to keep her aloft with a full load for a journey estimated to be more than four thousand miles and considered by many to be impossible. It was certainly true that no airship had ever flown even half that distance, and in this case there would be no return flight.

As modified, *L-59* was 750 feet long, with a diameter of 80 feet and a record-setting volume of almost 2.5 million cubic feet. She was powered by five Maybach HSL engines with a combined rating of 1,200 horsepower to give her a cruising speed of about 40 miles per hour during the more than four days required to cover the distance. The officer selected as her commander was Kapitänleutnant Ludwig Bockholt, described as less experienced in combat missions but quite capable of setting this kind of endurance record.

It was determined that the take-off point would be the airship base closest to East Africa, located in Bulgaria. Strasser himself was enthusiastic about the chances for success and knew that the flight would be good for morale in his ranks and would make a favorable impression on the Admiralty, to which he had to turn for his own funds and airship construction approvals.

The mission, which received approval from the Admiralty and the Kaiser himself at the end of the summer, was given the code name China Project to avoid the possibility that the Allies would get wind of it and make plans to intercept and shoot down the zeppelin en route. The voyage was not to be as the crow flies, since it was necessary to take circuitous routes to avoid any enemy encounters—first on the leg from Germany to Bulgaria and then on the long flight to East Africa.

On 21 November the ship rose into the air from its base at Friedrichshafen for the flight to Bulgaria and thence to her final destination. She was loaded with supplies for the beleaguered Lettow-Vorbeck, including more than 300,000 rounds of ammunition, thirty machine guns with boxes of cartridges and belts, sixty containers of medical supplies and bandages, and an assortment of combat knives, wireless parts, and clothing repair kits. Commander Bockholt had already failed in two attempts to get under way, frustrated by storms, high winds, and the fact that the ungainly ship, with its added length and bulk, was difficult to control under anything but ideal flying conditions.

From Bulgaria L-59 flew south over the Aegean and Crete to the north coast of Egypt. From there the biggest test of the ship's ability to survive lay in its performance over the vast Sahara, where the heat and glare were so intense that many crewmen had severe headaches and for a time were partially blinded. Currents of hot air caused severe and unexpected problems when they rocked the ship endlessly, making it difficult for the elevator man and wheelman to hold the ship on course. The heat and motion

167

also caused constant air sickness, even among men who had survived violent storms in the air without becoming ill.

Ironically, by the time *L-59* was halfway to her destination in East Africa, so many delays had occurred that the German forces were almost beyond help. Some of the troops under Lettow-Vorbeck had already been defeated and captured and the general had retreated to Mozambique, where he had the good fortune to capture some supplies from a Portuguese garrison. It was by then doubtful that the commander of *L-59* could have located the German force even if it had reached its planned objective. Bockholt's navigation proved surprisingly accurate despite his problems with the clumsy airship and the fact that he was flying over territory that was little known and in many places unmapped. For part of the way he followed the Nile, reaching the river's second cataract above Wadi Halfa, and then headed southward toward Khartoum—over desert, swamps, rain forests, mountains, and vast plains of grass. Had the ship been forced down because of storms, mechanical failures, gas leaks, or any other reason, her crew would have been totally isolated, forced to exist on the supplies she was carrying, most of which were munitions.

By the time *L-59* reached the midway point, estimated as being 130 miles west of Khartoum, on 23 November, the wireless operator received an unexpected message from the Admiralty's transmitter in Berlin:

CHINA PROJECT. ABORT OPERATIONS. ENEMY HAS SEIZED UNITS YOU WERE STAGING TO ASSIST. TURN BACK TO STARTING POINT.

Although the message was accepted as authentic, there was no way Commander Bockholt could confirm it. The Berlin radio was powerful enough to transmit all the way to Africa, but the

L-59's equipment was barely strong enough even to receive messages. Bockholt made the decision that he really was under orders to turn back and he did so. But he was astonished at the effect this news had on his men. Although up to this moment they had endured the tensions and hardships of the trip, they had been buoyed up by the magnitude of what they could accomplish once their destination had been reached. They did not even flinch at the thought that the mission called upon them to dismantle the airship, using the parts for constructing quarters, and remaining on the ground in East Africa as infantrymen in the fighting force under General von Lettow-Vorbeck. Now, however, the thought of ending in failure and yet still having to beat their way back home through winds and heat and possible enemy action was demoralizing.

L-59 did not return without incident. She had to contend not only with turbulent currents of rising hot air, but also with severe thunderstorms, constant headwinds, mechanical failures, and the loss of gas, all the time skirting enemy territory where ground and fighter plane attacks were possible. On 25 November she finally touched down in Bulgaria, having flown continuously for ninety-five hours and covering almost forty-five hundred miles.

Bockholt and his men were naturally discouraged and depressed. Yet it is doubtful that *L-59* would have reached German East Africa without having been attacked by enemy planes. The British had learned of the venture many weeks earlier through its intelligence network and had even pinpointed the date China Project would begin. Since the Allies occupied most of the territory around the small jungle perimeter held by Lettow-Vorbeck and his troops, there would have been no way of providing a defended air corridor when *L-59* had reached the point where she was to land. And she could not have remained long in the sky at an altitude above fighter plane and antiaircraft-artillery range.

Bockholt would have been no worse off, though, had he

169

continued. Only four months later, while under his command on a raiding mission to attack the British naval base at Malta, *L-59* was shot down in flames in the Strait of Otranto with no survivors.

Was the radio order to abort the African mission really from the Admiralty in Berlin?

There are two sides to the story. *The War in the Air*, an official World War I history published by the British government, accepts the order as being authentic and refers to it as a "wise step," asserting that the zeppelin's crew could never have located the scattered remnants of the German infantry forces. Even had she done so, continued this summary, her presence would have made the situation worse, not better, in part because the general would then have on his hands her crew of twenty-two men, all totally untrained as ground soldiers and likely to be susceptible to jungle diseases and conditions against which his regular troops were conditioned.

Later accounts of the flight insist that the British faked a report from Malta that caused the German high command to believe that General von Lettow-Vorbeck's cause was lost and his troops either surrendering or fleeing.

In either case, all accounts corroborate two facts: The general continued to hold out, even though retreating, and would have benefited by the medical supplies and munitions that had been loaded on *L-59*. The epic flight was one of the greatest achievements in zeppelin history and one of the reasons later advocates of the airship as a means of transportation continued in the 1920s and 1930s to campaign successfully for the development of dirigibles, particularly for peacetime uses.

THE DENOUEMENT

T he impressive technological ac-
complishment of *L-59* was largely lost on the German population
in late 1917. Even in military circles it was considered something
of a fluke that an airship, hastily modified and adapted for long-
range cruising, was able to remain airborne for so long and under
such trying conditions. The Germans focused their attention now
on building Gothas and other bombing planes and conducting
U-boat warfare, since it was too late in the season to plan zeppelin raids on England. Next year might be different, and Peter
Strasser concentrated on training his officers and men, improving
his ships and equipment, and hounding the high command for
approvals for new ships of the L-60 and L-70 class.

The high hopes he had for 1918 were dashed when, just five days after the start of the new year, his whole world seemed to explode in his face. On Saturday 5 January, in the late afternoon, Strasser was sitting in the small headquarters building at Ahlhorn conferring with the field commander when the air was shattered by explosions, followed by the insistent shriek of air-raid sirens. Dashing to the window, they looked out and saw a pillar of smoke and flame bursting through the roof of one of the four zeppelin sheds at the huge airship base.

"British planes have gotten through our defenses again," Strasser exclaimed grimly as the two officers raced outside, recalling several damaging raids that had been made by enemy seaplanes in the recent past.

This time, however, neither the Royal Navy nor the Royal Flying Corps was to blame. A gondola of *L-51* had somehow caught fire in the hangar while modifications and improvements were being made. In the explosions and fires that followed three of the four sheds went up in smoke, demolishing not only *L-51* but also sister ships *L-46*, *L-47*, and *L-58* and a Schütte-Lanz airship, *L-20*. Many of the nearby crew quarters were destroyed. A dozen men were killed and more than 130 injured during heroic attempts by all hands to save their ships.

Was this an accident? Sabotage? Or outright treason on the part of a German, one of a handful of malcontents who said that airship raids were suicidal and should be discontinued at all costs? No real clue was ever found and the disaster was forever listed on the records as mysterious.

This latest setback served to postpone all raids against the enemy until the night of 12 March, when Strasser once more led his zeppelins against the Midlands. This time he was in *L-63*, which had been commissioned only two days before. In extremely bad weather, accompanied by *L-53*, *L-54*, *L-61*, and

L-62, he proved that the Naval Airship Division had not yet lost its fangs.

As a follow-up performance three weeks later, he led another springtime raid, this time in *L-60*. His fleet of five ships cruised safely at an altitude of twenty thousand feet, the crews comfortably secure through the use of a new type of personal oxygen mask that did not cause nausea and blackouts. Not only did the Germans inflict heavy damage in the Midlands on this raid, but one ship, the new *L-61*, demonstrated the improved performance capabilities of the super-superzepps by transporting a full bomb load almost as far as Liverpool, on England's west coast. The new ships were powered by Maybach MBIV's, the first "altitude motors." They were much better insulated than previous models against the cold and were designed with a supplementary oxygen-injection system so that fuel was burned more smoothly and effectively in the rarefied atmosphere at twenty thousand feet.

The British defense was helpless and Strasser's ships were never in danger from either antiaircraft fire or night-fighter planes.

The success of these raids was dimmed, however, by two daring and effective enemy actions. On 10 May the *L-62* was attacked off Helgoland, the tiny, heavily fortified German base in the lower part of the North Sea, by a British F2a flying boat before she had time to climb to a safe altitude. She was shot down by the plane, which had purposely lain in the water waiting, her pilot knowing that the zeppelins frequently did not reach inaccessible heights until well over the North Sea on their route from Germany. All hands were lost with the ship.

Then, a little more than a month later, the zeppelin sheds at Tondern were brazenly attacked by a flight of Sopwith Camels under the leadership of Captain B. A. Smart, the man who had made history by taking off from the *Yarmouth*'s deck in August

173

1917 and shooting down the *L-23*. Two sheds were completely destroyed, along with their giant occupants, *L-54* and *L-60*.

Considering all these defeats and setbacks, it was incredible that Peter Strasser's influence was strong enough to keep obtaining approval for new zeppelins to add to the ever-diminishing fleet. He commanded so much respect and authority and was so dedicated in his personal zeal and sacrifices that the high command could not turn him down. In all, he had personally been responsible for constructing and commissioning more than eighty airships in a period of just over four years. With his boundless energy, he scurried from one great plant to another—from Friedrichshafen to Potsdam to Frankfurt-am-Main and Hamburg—checking out the minutest details and endlessly tightening up the schedules so that work continued around the clock, seven days a week.

With America in the war the Germans were losing ground heavily on almost all fronts. They had penetrated westward as far as Château-Thierry and almost within artillery range of Paris itself in June 1918. There, along the Marne River, they stood their ground until the end of the month. Then the French Tenth Army, bolstered by the U.S. First, Second, and Third divisions, smashed through the German lines. After a three-day battle the Germans were not only in full retreat but had the French and Americans in hot pursuit as they moved eastward, back toward the German border.

The last German offensive, the second Battle of the Marne, was over.

Although Strasser and his commanders were well aware that German infantry battalions were being cut to shreds on the ground, they refused to give up. During the first week in July, just before the Germans were to begin their gloomy retreat across the Marne River, the Führer der Luftschiff could be found testing out the newest and most formidable zeppelin in history, *L-70*, more than seven hundred feet long and capable, it was claimed, of making a round-trip crossing of the ocean.

"Now," said Strasser optimistically to Admiral Scheer one day, "we can cross the Atlantic, bomb America's East Coast, and force the United States to curtail the shipment of armament and pilots to France. The Americans, like the British, will have to devote much of their facilities and manpower to start building a home-defense system."

"We *could*," replied the admiral dejectedly. "But time is running out on Germany." He had only one more comment for Strasser, the officer he admired and respected perhaps more than any other man in the naval service. "I won't try to prevent further raids. I won't give you any negative orders. But I have a personal request: That you stay behind when *L-70* lifts off on her maiden raid."

Strasser smiled wanly. Then his intense dark eyes became deadly serious. "It is necessary, Sir, that I go. That is my destiny."

August fifth was a warm, humid day in Friedrichshafen. Strasser, who had restlessly sat out a period of unfavorable flying weather, decided to ignore a falling barometer and give the order everyone had long been waiting for.

"Ask Kapitänleutnant Lossnitzer to report to me. Prepare *L-70* for flight. Full bomb load."

Johann von Lossnitzer was *L-70*'s designated commander, a less experienced airshipman than Buttlar and several of the others but an officer of great promise. Strasser went over the charts meticulously with him, pointing out that he would be accompanied by four other excellent ships, the well-tried *L-53* and *L-56* and the capable new *L-63* and *L-65*.

Early in the afternoon of 5 August the gigantic *L-70* was ready to move out of her hangar. Nothing like her had ever been seen in the sky before. She had six of the new Maybach MBIV "altitude motors," capable of pushing her at speeds in excess of eighty miles per hour. They were designed so that they did not even begin to reach peak operating efficiency until the ship had climbed to 12,000 feet—about half of what she was capable of achieving if pushed. She had a hull volume of 2.2 million cubic feet and a useful overall lifting capacity of more than 85,000 pounds, including almost five tons of high-explosive bombs. One of the ship's most extraordinary features was the design of the sixteen gas cells, which were reportedly capable of being hit by incendiary bullets without exploding. The secret lay in layers of a puttylike material that was self-sealing when penetrated by bullets. Since hydrogen caught fire only when mixed with oxygen, the sealant prevented such a mixture from taking place and thus negated, or at least reduced, the threat of explosion.

Commander Lossnitzer climbed the ladder into the control gondola.

As he made his way forward, he paused abruptly in surprise. The dark figure in full naval uniform near the navigator's position was not his second-in-command. It was the Chief himself, Peter Strasser. That was Strasser's way. He seldom announced when he would go along on raids or on what ships. Often he himself did not decide until the last minute. It might be because a skipper was new or because a new class of ship was getting its maiden test, as in this case. He often chose to go along, too, when an intelligence report had indicated a special situation that might make it valuable for him to observe the raid.

Today he most certainly wanted to check out the performance of the new L-70 class in action, especially since Lossnitzer had appeared somewhat nervous. And just around midafternoon as the ships were ready to become airborne he could see that the weather was starting to act up, with tricky crosswinds lacing the field.

Strasser's presence, however, was never obtrusive, despite his four stripes. It was his practice to roam quietly about the ship on these occasions, always observing methods and performances with an eye to perfecting them, seldom to be critical of individuals. Sometimes during the monotony of a long, dark flight he would perch in a machine-gun position atop the bag, keeping some lonely gunner company during his vigil. Sometimes he would spend hours all but sitting on one of the Maybachs to listen to changes in the engine's purrings and protestings during changes in altitude or temperature.

Only once had Strasser been known to interfere directly with command responsibilities. That was when the zeppelin he had been riding had been severely crippled by flak over London and was barely able to make it back to the base. Through a kind of unwritten mutual consent, Strasser took over the controls during the landing when it looked as though disaster was imminent. He brought the battered ship down so skillfully that she suffered only minor damage to her gondolas.

The raiders were airborne with no difficulties, despite the nasty temperament of the weather, and reached the coast of England just after dusk. Strasser had hoped to sneak in at a lower-than-usual altitude to assure a more effective bomb run, then rise out of range quickly before the British could mount a real defense. But three of the ships were unexpectedly picked up by listening devices on the Leman Tail lightship off Yarmouth. Using a new quick-alert system, British fighter planes were promptly alerted, several of them already revved up for a possible attack. One of these was a de Havilland DH4, a two-seater piloted by Major Egbert Cadbury, with Captain R. J. Leckie at the Lewis gun in the observer's cockpit. Both men were pilots with considerable night-flying experience.

Cadbury left the Yarmouth aerodrome at 9:05 P.M., climbing rapidly through a cloud cover and emerging into clear air at twelve thousand feet. While climbing and well clear of land, Cadbury jettisoned some small bombs that were standard munitions on the DH4s, along with a reserve tank of fuel, to gain altitude more quickly. At 9:45 he sighted the three zeppelins—dark shapes against a cloud bank—just above him at seventeen thousand feet. He continued to climb, thus far unobserved, while Leckie readied his Lewis gun, loaded with incendiary shells and a new type of tracer bullet.

By 10:20, Cadbury was at sixteen thousand six hundred feet—still not seen by the Germans—approaching the nearest zeppelin almost head-on. She was the biggest he had ever seen. Even in the darkness she appeared to be an immense thundercloud that might descend on the small plane and swallow it up in the night. Just before scooting under the great bow of the airship, which seemed to be approaching like an express train, Cadbury veered slightly to port to avoid any trailing antennas or other obstructions that could foul and snap his wooden propeller instantly.

He did not know it then, but this was the Germans' biggest and newest airship, the *L-70*.

A few seconds later Leckie opened up with a steady burst, aiming at the bow but actually seeing his tracers pour into the hull about two-thirds of the way aft. So close was the airship now that, even in the darkness, he could see the shells ripping a large hole in the fabric. Then the hole burst into flames, as though someone had suddenly opened a gigantic furnace door.

The fire etched its way rapidly toward the stern, then forward toward the bow. All at once, what had until then been a ghostly black ship in the night sky became a red-hot cloud. (From a distance the other two zeppelin crews saw what looked like "a great cloud touched red at sunset by the dying sun." Then it was a gargantuan, elongated fireball.)

For a moment the *L-70* raised her bow, "as if in an effort to escape," said Cadbury later, "then plunged seaward in a blazing mass. The airship was completely consumed in less than a minute. We could see a huge petrol tank hurling away from the framework and falling in a blaze into a heavy layer of clouds about 7,000 feet below."

The other airships escaped and fled back to their bases. *L-53*'s time was running out, however, and she was shot down in flames off Terschelling five days later. *L-56*, *L-63*, and *L-65* remained on the ground until the end of the war and were decommissioned. All three were wrecked by German airship crews rather than being turned over to the Allies.

Thus ended the life of Peter Strasser and, with it, that of the Naval Airship Division. It was ironic that the end should have come at a time when Germany was so down on her knees that even the most patriotic officers and men no longer had any spirit left to toast their heroes, sung or unsung. Only a small cadre of men remained—like Hans von Schiller and Ernst Lehmann and Hugo Eckener, who would later revive the airship's glory and look back on Strasser as one of the pioneers who made it possible.

There is no doubt that Strasser's accomplishments were formidable. It is within the realm of possibility that Germany might have greatly prolonged the war with airship raids had the Kaiser and the German high command had the foresight to launch the military zeppelin program two or three years earlier than it did, build stockpiles of nonflammable gas such as helium, and develop at the same time more accurate bombsights and more effective bombs. At the very least, the Germans might have found themselves in a far better bargaining position when it came time for an armistice.

Even as it was, Strasser's airships accomplished one major

tactical objective: by the end of the war, they were tying down something like twenty-five thousand officers and men in the British Home Guard, forcing the Allies to channel thousands of artillery pieces and shells to England instead of the front lines, and hog-tying more than a dozen Royal Flying Corps defense squadrons, along with almost two hundred planes and nearly three thousand pilots and maintenance personnel.

Over and beyond that, the zeppelins disrupted vital war-plant production during blackouts, disorganized communications, and oftentimes shattered British morale. Their basic strategic importance was certainly far, far greater than the measurement of the few million dollars' worth of actual damage they managed to inflict on enemy installations. It is astonishing indeed that the bizarre, ungainly, and highly vulnerable brainchild of the aging Ferdinand von Zeppelin, as adapted by the brilliant and dedicated Peter Strasser, could ever have found such a significant niche in the military history of the world.

"**P**ort engines, up flank speed!"

"Starboard engines, hold standard. Valve cells four and five!"

It was three-thirty in the morning of Thursday 3 September 1925, and in the control cabin of the huge cigar-shaped dirigible *Shenandoah* her skipper, Lieutenant Commander Zachary Lansdowne, was worried. No matter how he adjusted throttle and ballast, he could not keep the 680-foot airship steady in the mounting turbulence over southeastern Ohio. He was relieved to see that his second-in-command, Lieutenant Commander Charles B. Rosendahl, was just coming on duty as navigator. He would need all the help he could get that night trying to beat due east toward the airship base at Lakehurst.

Rosendahl, who had been asleep in his hammock as the storm mounted, was surprised to learn that the wind was gusting to seventy miles per hour. "Line squall, Sir," explained the helmsman. "We picked her up an hour ago and can't seem to shake ourselves loose no matter what altitude or direction we try."

The *Shenandoah* was headed completely in the opposite direction from her intended destination, forced to do so to keep her nose directly into the wind. Whenever the men in the control cabin tried to change course, the ship would buck and vibrate dangerously and threaten to go totally out of control. The cabin itself—a thin, streamlined shell of aluminum about the size of a railroad passenger car that dangled under the helium-filled bag of the rigid airship—was in danger of being wrenched loose from the cables and struts that held it in place and dashing the officers and men to their deaths three thousand feet below. The situation could not have been more precarious.

The *Shenandoah* represented the bid of the United States Navy to become an airborne, as well as seagoing, arm of the military service shortly after the end of World War I. Although the huge German zeppelin fleet amassed by Peter Strasser had not been able to realize his ambitious goal of bombing England into submission, it had achieved astonishing results on many occasions. A number of air-minded navy top brass had been greatly impressed. They could see the potential of a naval dirigible armada as a valuable support system for the surface fleet for a number of purposes, including far-ranging observation, the quick transportation of supplies and personnel, and even bombing raids at very high altitudes. They realized that America had one major advantage in airship technology that had been denied the Germans: plentiful sources of helium, which would not catch fire or explode no matter how many incendiary bullets were pumped into it.

Thus it was that, at the beginning of the 1920s, the United States Navy made arrangements with the Allied command to obtain one of the few zeppelins that had not been shot down in flames or purposely wrecked on the ground. Using this as a life-size prototype, the navy made certain improvements, redesigned the gas cells to compensate for the lifting differential between helium and hydrogen, and perfected on the drawing boards a brand-new superairship to be named *Shenandoah*. She was launched with much fanfare in September 1923, an Americanized version of Strasser's L-50 and L-60 zeppelin types.

Zachary Lansdowne had been selected as commander because his credentials qualified him as the most experienced officer in the navy in lighter-than-air craft. Besides having studied airship design and control for years, he had also taken many flights on British airships, including the *R-34* on an unprecedented round-trip flight across the Atlantic in 1919.

It was ironic that Lansdowne and his officers and men should now find themselves in such a life-threatening situation. The commander had, on numerous occasions, pointed out to navy brass that airships were extremely susceptible to bad weather. They could ice up so heavily in subfreezing temperatures that they could become sheathed in ice and unmanageable. At the other extreme, when operated in very hot regions under a glaring sun, the helium could expand suddenly and rip the cells. During gales, the enormous horizontal expanse of the hull could prevent maneuvering, while sudden gusts could tear the fragile envelope. And even under the best of conditions, ships had to be readied for takeoff with great care and then brought back to earth firmly and skillfully to avoid combinations of dead-air pockets and wind shear that could dash the gondolas and keel to the ground suddenly and with disastrous results.

Only the week before, Lansdowne had protested as rigorously

as he could to the secretary of the navy that the navy was pursuing a suicidal route. In its eagerness to promote its new prize and win plaudits for its farsightedness in the air, the navy was scheduling cross-country flights without obtaining reliable meteorological data in advance. High on his lists of regions to avoid were the Midwestern plains near the Great Lakes where line squalls were frequent and often too local to be reported by weather stations.

As Rosendahl came on duty that night and tried as quickly as possible to evaluate the situation and assist his commander, he could sense that they were in deep trouble. The instruments could not function with all the bucking and careening that was taking place in the control cabin. The altimeter needle and the bubble in the inclinometer shuttled crazily from one reading to another totally different one. The radio operator, supposedly blessed with the very latest in wireless equipment, could neither pick up weather reports nor get through to any stations for information. The helmsman could not press his weight against the wheel forcefully enough, even with the help of one of the enginemen, to change the settings on the huge tail fins.

For the next hour Lansdowne and Rosendahl tried vainly to keep the ship on a proper heading and maintain an altitude of about three thousand feet. It was useless. The six three-hundred-horsepower Packard engines, though running at full speed, were not powerful enough to permit a change of course. Inside the great hull overhead (covered with taut silken fabric) the sound of creaking aluminum girders and struts torn loose echoed as though on the inside of a gargantuan drum. Inspecting the interior from a position along the keel, Rosenthal noted with anxiety that the interior framework was twisting and straining so badly that the skin alternately became drum-tight, then wrinkled like the outside of a twisted sausage.

184

At about the same time, checking the pear-shaped aluminum engine gondolas, the chief machinist's mate was concerned about the severe jolting and whipping of the gondolas. Not only could they tear loose from the struts holding them outside the framework, but there was also an ever-present danger that fuel lines would rupture and cause a fire when spraying gasoline splashed against red-hot engine metal. He was concerned, too, that there was a critical risk of breakdowns if the engines continued too long to run at flank speed. The *Shenandoah* was actually going nowhere at all at this point. Headed into the wind, which averaged sixty-five knots or more, the ship was actually standing still in relationship to its position above the ground from one hour to the next. (The next day, in fact, farmers in Noble County, Ohio, reported that they had been awakened by aircraft engines overhead during the early morning hours and were astonished when the sound, alternating with the howl of the wind, never moved on and could be heard for an hour or more in the same location.)

In the control cabin another officer, Lieutenant Joseph B. Anderson, had an equally frustrating job as he tried to valve gas, a procedure used to maintain the equilibrium of an airship when the wind, temperature changes, and other forces were threatening to throw her off balance. The ship had been constructed with eighteen gas-escape valves, but the navy had ordered eight of these removed to lessen the tendency of helium—a very valuable commodity—to leak slightly but continuously. This not only made Anderson's task more difficult but struck him now as being an error that could be fatal.

The crisis came at 5:25 A.M., just before dawn, when the *Shenandoah* was battling the gale at twenty-six hundred feet. It was difficult for those in the control cabin to tell what happened exactly, but suddenly the needle on the altimeter stopped wobbling and shot up as though activated by a steel spring.

"Good God!" exclaimed Rosendahl. "Look at our rate of climb!"

In a matter of seconds the altimeter registered an ascent of more than two thousand feet as the airship knifed into a gigantic column of warm air rising skyward. Men who were standing at control posts staggered as the deck seemed to rise like an express elevator and they felt their legs literally buckling under them.

"Trim ship! Trim ship!" commanded Lansdowne, his breath almost knocked out of him by the vicious upward motion. "Andy, valve number six and eight cells—fast! Rosie, release ballast aft and get her nose down!"

By now the ship was careening crazily to port, her blunt nose still rising skyward like a dolphin about to stand on its tail. Lansdowne screamed for more power from the port engines, to lessen the list in that direction. But they were already straining at the full and could deliver no more. These procedures occupied only seconds, yet they seemed like an eternity. By the time a modicum of balance was attained again, the needle on the altimeter was wavering at forty-eight hundred feet. Looking outside the cabin at masses of gray thunderheads in the breaking dawn, they could see with relief that they were now almost stabilized again. But they did not like the looks of the repeated bolts of lightning that flashed all around the ship.

Now there was another problem to contend with. Although Lieutenant Anderson thought he was valving effectively, the ship had begun climbing out of control again—to fifty-five hundred feet, then six thousand, then sixty-five hundred. He suddenly realized with dismay that two valves were not functioning at all but were hopelessly jammed. The cabin began swinging wildly again, making it difficult, if not impossible, to handle the controls.

"All hands, emergency posts! Emergency posts!" shouted

Lansdowne into the ship's speaking tube. By now his orders could scarcely be heard above the whine of the wind and the severe creaking of aluminum girders and the whipping of steel cables. "Rosie," he said calmly, "we've got to get her nose down fast. If we don't, we'll break up for sure. I'm not sure my messages are getting through at all, so run aft and have the men jettison everything you can to lighten the tail—water, fuel, supplies—I don't care what goes overboard."

The altimeter was now showing seventy-two hundred feet and rising.

As Rosendahl left the control cabin and stumbled along the catwalk heading aft, clutching the handrails to keep from being hurled loose, he was shocked to hear the unbelievable hissing, booming, crunching, echoing, and reverberating noises inside the hull itself. There was a sound like the roaring of surf mingled with sharp snapping noises, and protesting squeals like those he recalled from a voyage on a windjammer in a full gale.

At that instant, he later recalled, he fully realized that the *Shenandoah* was doomed. How many of them—if any—could survive a crash of such deadly dimensions?

In the control cabin Lieutenant Anderson heard Commander Lansdowne ordering the operator in the radio shack to send out an SOS—a futile order since no radio contact was possible. Then Lansdowne turned to him and shouted: "We've got to valve gas and get her down lower. You'll have to hand-valve, Andy, if those damned valves can't be unstuck. So go topside and blow all cells. Commandeer as many men as you need and tell them I said so!"

"Aye, aye, Sir!" Anderson's quick compliance saved his life. As he left the control cabin and swung onto the ladder leading to the catwalk, he heard a sudden scream from the wheelman that the cable had snapped. This was followed by a tearing, snapping noise like the ripping of many layers of fabric at the same time. The voices trailed strangely away at the same instant. When Anderson looked back he saw, in horror, nothing but a great open void and far below the streamlined, silvery shape of the control cabin plunging downward toward the earth.

At that moment, looking in the other direction, he saw Commander Rosendahl making his perilous way along the forward part of the same catwalk, near the bow. "The control cabin!" he shouted in a voice that echoed weirdly inside the envelope. "It just tore loose! Lansdowne, the others—they've all gone down with it!"

Whatever response Rosendahl might have tried to make was obliterated as they were shaken by a tremendous crash. All around them aluminum girders were buckling. Their eardrums were split by the high-pitched, ripping scream of the hull's fabric as it was torn to shreds by the fury of wind and slashing girders. The *Shenandoah* plunged to earth at last in a massive tangle of wreckage.

Lieutenant Commander Rosendahl's ordeal was not over yet, however. Through one of the strangest twists of fate in the often strange history of airships, the entire bow section of the *Shenandoah* was torn loose and started to rise back into the air. Aboard this great bulbous nose were Rosendahl and seven other officers and men, clinging to what was in effect a huge free balloon, rising and falling in the air currents. When it rose to what he judged to be more than two thousand feet, he realized that their only hope lay in valving off gas from what seemed to be three helium gas cells in the tangle of girders and fabric overhead. Coolly and deliberately, with the knowledge that their survival depended upon their every move, four of the survivors inched their way along cables and twisted framework, hand over hand, to the locations of two of the valves and began the dangerous task of leaking off helium. Too little and they might never get down in time. Too much and the wreckage would plunge earthward with deadly force.

While this attempt was in progress, Rosendahl supervised the preparation of makeshift ground anchors, which they made from pieces of trailing rope to which they attached chunks of metal and fabric—anything that could snag on trees and bushes below and keep them from being swept along by the wind. By the time they were down to about two hundred feet above the ground these proved effective. The nose came to rest in a grove of trees, still whipping violently in the wind.

Of the thirty-seven officers and men aboard the *Shenandoah*, thirteen were killed in the crash of the control car, including Lieutenant Commander Lansdowne, and two others died in the crash of the hull and the nose section. As for Rosendahl and the rest, all but one suffered relatively minor injuries and were able to go back on duty within a matter of days.

Thus ended the short, controversial life of the first American "zeppelin." It was as though Fregatenkapitän Peter Strasser had risen out of his untimely grave to warn the United States Navy that it could not hope to copy his handiwork and that of the old Count Ferdinand von Zeppelin so easily. They would have to pay a price, just as he had paid a price. And as all future developers of airships would do—German, British, French, Italian, and American.

The story of the *Shenandoah* illustrates the point that the lighter-than-air giants of the sky have historically defied all attempts at taming and harnessing by man, in war and peace alike. Unlike artillery and ships and planes, they even resisted acquisition as spoils of war. At the close of World War I there were nine zeppelins in the Germans' hangars. Four of these met an anonymous fate, destroyed "by persons unknown," in order to prevent their falling into the hands of the Allied victors. The remaining airships (*L-61*, *L-64*, *L-71*, *LZ-113*, and *LZ-120*) and two passenger airships, *Bodensee* and *Nordstern*, were restored by the navy and delivered by civilian crews to various airfields as specified in official truce agreements.

The Allies intended now to take advantage of Germany's recognized superiority in the design and operation of rigid airships for their own advantage, as well as to make it impossible for the Germans to develop peacetime airship travel. But they failed to take into consideration their almost complete lack of training and practical experience in this field. The result was to be sheer disaster.

L-61, *LZ-120*, and *Bodensee* were delivered to Italy. The *L-61*, rechristened *Italia*, was the first catastrophe. Putting on a grand show for the king of Italy, the commander threw open all throttles without considering the force and direction of the wind. The resultant crash completely wrecked the ship and killed or injured most of the crew. *LZ-120*, which had last been commanded by the able Ernst Lehmann, met a more passive, but equally dismal, fate—smashed while being deflated in its hangar. Only the *Bodensee*, renamed the *Esperia*, survived to carry out a number of voyages over the Mediterranean before being decommissioned in 1928.

The French were awarded *L-72*, *LZ-113*, and *Nordstern*, along with a later ship that was still being built, was christened the *Dixmude*, and made a number of voyages under the able command of a French naval officer, Jean du Plessis de Grenedan. One was a long flight to the Sahara that set an endurance record for airships of almost 119 hours in the air. Her fame was nevertheless short-lived. In the early hours of 21 December 1923 she was returning from another long flight, this time to Algeria, at a low altitude. The Germans had advised the French that this airship, the most advanced ever built, was designed for high-altitude flight and, because of her size and vulnerability to wind and lightning, should never be flown through storms. The French government, eager to set a new record, had charted a low-altitude route over the Mediterranean. Although du Plessis, reporting that the area was turbulent with thunderstorms, vigorously objected to this strategy, he was overruled by his superiors.

The airship was never seen again. Eleven days after she had taken off, Sicilian fishermen hauled in their nets to discover, to their horror, pieces of wreckage and the bodies of two men. One was that of du Plessis. The loss of fifty officers and men was a national disaster that marked the end of France's rigid-airship program. The *Nordstern*, which had been renamed *Méditerranée*, was taken out of service immediately and later dismantled, and the *LZ-113* was used for a time for study and research.

Admiral Reinhard von Scheer, former chief of the German high seas fleet, had written in his memoirs of the war: "The technique of airship navigation was so greatly promoted by the experience of the war that airship transport in peacetime will be greatly benefited and the invention of Count Zeppelin will be preserved as a step forward in civilization."

His prophecy was not to come true, certainly not in the hands of the Allies. Hans von Schiller explained, with understandable bitterness: "If the technique of airship navigation was retarded for years by the imprudent attitude of the Entente [the peace agreement], this was because the victorious powers had insufficient experience in the management of the technically perfect instruments and refused to allow us to continue the development. Thus a large part of the loss of airships abroad is to be blamed on the Treaty of Versailles. The situation of German airship navigation was hopeless."

If it had not been for a handful of dedicated airshipmen, most notably Hugo Eckener, the history of the rigid airship would have ended completely by the middle of the 1920s. As soon after the war as early 1919, he laid plans to make a transoceanic voyage with a new ship, *L-72*, which had just been completed and not yet given over to the Allies. He had gathered a crew to train at the airship's base in the Lowental hangar, near Friedrichshafen, when the interim German government prohibited the venture and placed armed guards around the hangar to assure compliance. Eckener's disappointment reached its climax when, in early July, the British made airship history by crossing from England to Montreal and back in the new *R-34*—an almost exact copy of the ill-fated German Zeppelin *L-33* that had been forced down on British soil during the war and captured intact.

Eckener persisted in his efforts to preserve what was left of the German Zeppelin organization and hit upon a plan to construct a new airship and offer it to the United States, which had been entitled to one of the former German zeppelins under the peace treaty. The airship that resulted, using the most advanced technology of the day, was the *ZR-3*, completed in mid-1924. She was flown from Germany to Lakehurst, New Jersey, in October and greeted by many thousands of Americans. Renamed *Los Angeles*, she was assigned to the U.S. Navy and went into active service.

Hugo Eckener's persistence and dedication paid off as he began planning for the construction of a new German airship in 1925, when the Treaty of Locarno rescinded restrictions that limited the size of ships that Germany could build. But he had to stump the length and breadth of his country for two years on an exhaustive lecture- and fund-raising tour before he could raise two and a half million marks. Although this was only half the amount needed, he began construction and was able to persuade the impoverished government to come up with the rest of the money on the assumption that the new airship would give a big boost to both the economy and morale of the nation.

The airship that resulted was the *Graf Zeppelin*, designed by the world's most brilliant airship engineer, Ludwig Dürr, who had started with Count Ferdinand von Zeppelin in 1899. Measuring 775 feet in length, 100 feet in width, and 110 feet in height, she was the largest airship ever built and, in the long run, the most successful in peacetime history. She left her hangar for the first time on 13 September 1928, under Eckener's command. Some three weeks later, she began the first transoceanic voyage ever made by an airship that carried paying passengers.

The *Graf Zeppelin* was to log more than a million miles on flights around the world under the command of some of the most prominent men in airship history. Had the Germans retained control over the Zeppelin works and organizations they had developed, the history of the airship—the dirigible—might have been completely different. The problems generally evolved because other nations tried their hand in a technology that was not familiar and in which their engineers and commanders had very little experience. The examples of the Italians and the French were paralleled by those of the British. Exultant over having made the first transoceanic crossing in 1919, England later began a program to build new superairships. The *R 101* was one of these. She was 777 feet long and 131 feet in diameter. From the very start, however, the ship failed to live up to expectations. The engines, designed originally for railway locomotives, were too heavy and too weak and vibrated so badly they could not be run at maximum speeds. The dope used for treating the fabric of the enormous envelope set up such a chemical reaction that all the material had to be scrapped and replaced. And the controls were so awkward and poorly designed that the airship was prone to taking unexpected nosedives. When it was discovered that the gasbags were chafing against the metal girders, causing leaks, the British simply tied wads of padding around the protruding ribs rather than undergo the cost of redesign.

On 4 October 1930, after many delays, the *R-101* was ready to fly from Carington, near Bedford, England, to Karachi, India, with a landing en route beside the Suez Canal. That evening fifty-four people boarded the ship—forty-two crew members and twelve distinguished passengers. The first problem arose when the engines refused to start without rounds of ominous sputterings and wheezings. Then, as the ship backed away from the mooring mast, the nose dipped unexpectedly, necessitating the release of a vast spray of ballast water that thoroughly doused the cheering throng below.

All over southeastern England crowds gathered, despite bad weather, to try to get a glimpse of the airship as it headed toward France. Several onlookers reported later that they were dismayed at how sluggish the huge monster seemed, as though the engines could not cope with her size and bulk. Within an hour of departure, the aft engine failed, leaving the ship to struggle through a rising storm with only four. The *R-101* never rose more than a thousand feet, barely missing some high buildings and almost within range of the spray from white waves rolling across the English Channel.

As the airship crossed into northern France the weather worsened noticeably, with gusts of forty to fifty knots—twice what meteorologists had forecast. By now the rolling and pitching was so severe that crew members had a difficult time handling the controls at all.

Shortly after two in the morning the radio operator exchanged messages with Le Bourget airport and confirmed the fact that the airship was somewhere near Beauvais, eighty miles north of Paris. At about this time the helmsman in the control car was startled to sight a dark object protruding out of the mist on the port side of the airship and only yards away. It was the spire of Beauvais Cathedral. He barely had time to shout an alarm when the airship lurched crazily, shuddered from stem to stern, and echoed with an ear-splitting roar as gas escaped through cells that had been ripped wide open. The nose had plunged into a wooded ridge. The *R-101* exploded almost instantly.

All but eight men died at the scene, and two of them died later of their burns. Among the dead were high British, Indian, and Australian officials and the designers and chief builders of the *R-101*. So overwhelmed were the British by this tragedy that they dismantled the downed dirigible's sister ship, *R-100*, canceled their ambitious design and construction program, and bowed out of the great airship race forever.

That left only the Germans and the Americans. The latter persisted for a few years, despite what had happened to the *Shenandoah*, largely because of the leadership of a few dedicated airshipmen and the fact that the United States had plentiful supplies of helium, which was nonflammable. The picture was to change abruptly.

In the late evening of 3 April 1933 the Navy's newest airship, the *Akron*, flew into a storm off the New Jersey coast and was forced down. Even with the elevators in the up position and the engines at full throttle the ship, then called "the biggest and most technologically refined airship the world had yet seen," hit the water at high speed and broke up. Of the seventy-six people aboard, only three survived. Among the dead was Rear Admiral William A. Moffett, a prime mover of the navy's airship program.

That left only the *Macon*, which had been christened just a few weeks earlier by the admiral's wife. The public and navy officials alike now urged that the United States abandon its dirigible program. Despite the outcry, the *Macon* continued in service during 1933 and 1934, used largely for scouting purposes with the fleet. Using fighter planes that could be lowered on "sky hooks" under the belly of the ship, the *Macon* could survey as much as 130,000 square miles of ocean in a single day. On 12 February 1935 the *Macon* was cruising off Point Sur, California, under the command of Lieutenant Commander Herbert V. Wiley, one of the survivors of the *Akron* disaster. She was suddenly struck by a gust of heavy wind that wrenched loose a previously damaged fin, ripping the internal fabric and deflating the gas cells in the tail. Some twenty-four minutes after the accident the ship fell into the sea and slowly began to sink. Mercifully, since the water was warm (in contrast to the freezing waters into which the *Akron* crashed) only two of the eighty-three crewmen aboard lost their lives. But the loss of the *Macon* was the final straw and the U.S. Navy washed its hands of the rigid-airship program.

Now, in the whole wide world there was only one major rigid airship in active service: the famous *Graf Zeppelin*. Why had the Germans been so successful, even with limited budgets and restrictions, when all other nations had failed?

Dr. Hugo Eckener had one more ambition: to build an even greater airship and prove to the world that Germany was on the comeback trail. Work on this new superzepp, the *Hindenburg*, had begun in late 1931 under the supervision of Eckener's son Knut. There were soon to be enormous problems, but this time they were political. The appointment of Adolf Hitler as the chancellor of Germany in January 1933 placed Eckener in a precarious position. He was an avowed anti-Nazi, thus far spared from persecution because of his stature as a world-honored figure and hence a boon to the propaganda program. The Nazis took over complete control of the airship organizations and personnel. They formed the German Zeppelin Airline Company, with Eckener's right-

hand man Ernst Lehmann as technical manager and superinten-
dent of flight. Eckener was little more now than a figurehead.

The huge new airship soared aloft on the maiden flight in
March 1933, its hundred-foot-high vertical fins emblazoned
with black swastikas set in a white circle against a red background. There was no doubt who was in charge. Within a few
weeks the *Hindenberg* had been pressed into service, flying
throughout Germany dropping leaflets supporting Hitler's plan
to remilitarize the Rhineland. Eckener referred to this as a "mad
flight" and was deeply critical of Lehmann's willingness to cooperate with the Nazis. When Joseph Goebbels, Hitler's minister
of propaganda, heard about this, he raged: "Dr. Eckener has
alienated himself from the nation. In the future his name may no
longer be mentioned in newspapers, nor may his picture be
used."

The first passenger flight of the *Hindenburg* was a round-trip to
Rio de Janeiro at the end of March 1936. During the course of the
next year, the airship made a number of long-distance voyages,
winning great respect and admiration for the new Germany.
There was only one serious flaw in the operation: Dr. Eckener had
intended to fill the gas cells in the *Hindenburg* with nonflammable
helium in place of hydrogen and had all but completed plans to
purchase supplies from the United States. But the Nazis were
imposing severe trade restrictions on dealings with a number of
countries and had forbidden the importation of certain materials
from the United States, including helium.

Two new zeppelins were scheduled for construction. The first,
LZ-130, would accommodate 100 passengers and the other,
LZ-131, would have space for 150. Dr. Eckener hoped that the
transatlantic schedules would be complemented by flights clear
across the Pacific within a few years. The future seemed so bright
that he had already interested the United States in forming an

international zeppelin company and in establishing commercial airship bases near several American cities, including Washington, D.C.

The first 1937 flight of the *Hindenburg* to Lakehurst, New Jersey, was scheduled to leave Germany's new Rhein–Main World Airport on 3 May. At eight-fifteen that evening it rose majestically into the air to the music of a brass band playing the German national anthem and the Nazi *Horst Wessel* rallying song. The ship was under the command of an experienced captain, Max Pruss, who had served in zeppelins during World War I and was a former captain of the *Graf Zeppelin*. He was joined by four other zeppelin commanders and at least twenty extra crewmen who were on board as part of the training program for future duty on the two new airships then being built.

At the last minute, Ernst Lehmann decided to make the flight as a way of allaying fears communicated in a letter from an American woman in Milwaukee to the German ambassador in Washington. She urged the Germans to open and search all mail and packages sent to the airport for delivery aboard the *Hindenburg*. "The Zeppelin is going to be destroyed by a time bomb during its flight to another country," she wrote. "Please believe my words as the truth, so that no one later will have cause for regret."

Was this a crank letter? Lehmann thought so and decided that his presence on board would be a positive sign that everything was in order.

The Atlantic crossing proved tedious and unusually long because the airship was slowed by persistent headwinds. The anticipated glory of an arrival in America and a flight over New York City before heading across the Hudson River to the airfield at Lakehurst was dimmed by continuing delays and the threat of severe thunderstorms in the area. The *Hindenburg* did pass over

New York, as well as Boston, and was then forced to make a wide circle as far away as the Delaware River before the weather broke long enough for Pruss to be advised that he should make a dash for Lakehurst and set the airship down.

The rest of the story is history in the most dramatic sense. The arrival of Germany's largest and proudest airship was witnessed—despite the delay and the bad weather—by a large crowd of spectators, relatives and friends of the passengers, and an assortment of journalists, photographers, and radio announcers. On the ground, commander Charles Rosendahl, commanding officer of the naval air station at Lakehurst and a survivor of the *Shenandoah* disaster, later reported that the landing seemed to be proceeding "routinely" at 7:25 P.M. on Thursday 6 May. The bow handling lines had been tossed down and grabbed by ground crews. The airship was stationary at about seventy-five feet. And everyone on board was preparing to debark with no sense of impending doom.

What happened was so sudden and totally unexpected that few of the survivors were ever able to describe what happened. Within a matter of seconds, the huge dark mass of the hull had turned into a blazing inferno and people were tumbling out of it onto the ground. It was nothing short of miraculous that sixty-two people survived the holocaust and only thirty-six lost their lives. Commander Max Pruss was among those who lived. But Ernst Lehmann, who had survived numerous sorties and raids in World War I zeppelins, was not so fortunate. He died of severe burns twenty-four hours after the disaster.

His last words, as he was led away in shock with his clothes on fire and his flesh seared, had been "I don't understand it!"

Few other airshipmen did either. The only thing they knew for certain was that the rigid airship was now nothing more than a ghost from the past.

GLOSSARY

Familiarity with these terms will be useful in reading about zeppelins and the part they played in the history and outcome of World War I.

AA, ACK-ACK. *See* antiaircraft.

ADMIRALTY. The official office and/or building in London of the British Commission for Naval Affairs. Also the high-ranking naval officers who were members.

AEROPLANE. British spelling for *airplane*.

AFT, AFTER. At, close to, or toward the stern of a craft.

AIRSHIP. A self-propelled lighter-than-air craft with means of control.

AIRSPEED. The forward velocity of an aircraft through air.

ALTIMETER. An instrument graduated and calibrated to indicate the distance above sea level or terrain.

ALTITUDE MOTOR. A World War I aircraft motor designed and built by the Germans to function at great heights, generally above 15,000 feet.

ANTIAIRCRAFT. Pertaining to artillery designed for use against aircraft.

ARMAMENT. The arms and equipment of a military vessel, aircraft, or unit.

BALANCE. State of equilibrium.

BALLAST. Heavy material carried in a vessel or aircraft to provide stability.

BALLONET. A compartment or bag containing air or gas to control buoyancy and maintain shape in an airship.

BALLOON. A bag made of light material and containing hot air or gas, capable of rising into the air but not powered by motors.

BLIMP. A small, nonrigid airship, powered or nonpowered; especially one used for observation purposes.

BOMB. A projectile filled with a bursting charge and exploded by impact, a fuse, or otherwise.

BOMBSIGHT. An instrument on an airship or airplane used for sighting on a target below.

BOW. The front end of a craft.

BUOYANCY. The power to float or rise.

CATWALK. A narrow walkway, especially along the keel section of an airship, that provides access from one section to another.

CEILING. The maximum altitude at which an aircraft can operate under specified conditions.

CELL. The flexible, balloon-shaped nonrigid container in an airship that contains hydrogen, helium, or other lifting gas.

CLOUD CAR. A device invented by the Germans in which an observer is lowered on a cable below an airship for observation purposes.

COMPASS. An instrument for determining direction by means of a freely rotating magnetized needle that indicates magnetic north. Airship compasses compensate for motion and the presence of large masses of metal, such as engines and bomb loads.

CONTROL CAR. The cabin, usually affixed to the belly of an airship, that contains instruments and controls necessary for flight.

CONTROL GONDOLA. Control car.

COVER. The skin or envelope of a zeppelin, dirigible, or other rigid airship, made of lightweight fabric or other material and encompassing the skeleton and hull of the ship.

CUBIC FOOTAGE. Measurement of the amount of space in units (1' × 1' × 1'), used to designate the volume inside the hull of an airship.

DE HAVILLAND. Designation for a popular fighting plane used by the Allies during World War I, named for its designer.

DECOMMISSION. To take out of commission or use, said of military craft no longer in active service.

DELAG. Deutsche Luffschiffahrt-Aktien-Gesellschaft, the airship design and manufacturing company established by Count Ferdinand von Zeppelin in Germany in 1909.

DIRIGIBLE. An airship designed and fitted so that it can be directed, controlled, or steered in flight.

DOCKING LINES. Ropes and other lines used to help control an airship on the ground during landing and takeoff.

DOCKING RAILS. Metal rails running into and out of sheds housing airships. The rails held in place trolleys to which were affixed lines from airships to control them when leaving or entering the sheds.

DOPE. A chemical solution brushed or sprayed on the skin of airships to tauten and waterproof the fabric.

DRIFT. Lateral movement relationship to the ground caused by air currents and wind.

DURALUMIN. A very light-weight aluminum alloy developed in Germany at about the time Count von Zeppelin was constructing his first airships.

DYNAMIC LIFT. The extra lift, over and beyond that of the gas cells, given to an airship when the engines help it to plane slightly upward during flight.

EARS. Nickname for acoustical devices invented during World War I to detect the sound of aircraft engines approaching in the sky. *See also* Orthophone.

ELEVATOR. An adjustable horizontal surface at the tail of an airship, operated remotely from the control car and used to incline the tail (and, in reverse, the nose) upward or downward in flight.

ENGINE CAR. The gondola, pod, or other unit containing an engine in an airship.

ENGINE POD. Engine car.

ENGINEER. On an airship, an individual in charge of an engine, motor, or other mechanical equipment.

ENGINEMAN. An individual assigned to running, maintaining, or supervising the performance of an engine on an airship.

ENVELOPE. *See* Cover.

EXECUTIVE OFFICER. Usually the second in command on an airship; his duties are complementary to those of the commander and usually designated by the latter.

FABRIC. *See* Cover.

FIN. An adjustable vertical surface at the tail of an airship, operated remotely from the control car and used to turn the ship right or left.

FLANK SPEED. The maximum possible speed of a vessel or airship.

FLARE. Incendiary device dropped from airplanes or airships to light up the ground or airspace below. These could be set off upon release, by altitude pressure, or upon contact. Some were attached to parachutes to provide constant, sustained light while moving earthward.

FORE. At, close to, or toward the bow of a vessel or airship.

FREE LIFT. A term used by the Germans when dropping water ballast to provide extra lift when needed.

FREGATENKAPITÄN. A German naval aviation rank during World War I equivalent to that of rear admiral.

FRIEDRICHSHAFEN. A port on Lake Constance (Bodensee) in southwestern Germany; the site of Count Zeppelin's early experiments with airships and later the location of a major zeppelin construction works.

GANGWAY. A narrow walkway, generally along the keel of an airship, that permits access to various units of the ship along its route. *See also* Catwalk.

GAS CELL. Huge nonrigid bags of rubber or fabric that contained the hydrogen, helium, or other gas used in airships. These were affixed in place by cables and netting and contained valves to control the flow and release of gas.

GIRDER. Very lightweight beams of aluminum, duralumin, wood, or other materials used to keep the long hull of an airship rigid and assure that it retained its streamlined shape.

GONDOLA. A control, passenger, or engine compartment suspended below an airship, generally by cables or struts, and streamlined to lessen wind resistance.

GOTHA. A giant bomber built during World War I and named after the industrial city in central Germany where it was initially produced.

GROSS LIFT. The total lifting power of the hydrogen, helium, or other gas in an airship based on a formula taking into account the difference between the lesser weight of the gas and the greater weight of the same amount of air displaced at any given altitude.

HANGAR. A large shed used to house an airship or other aircraft.

HEAVIER-THAN-AIR CRAFT. Any aircraft weighing more than the air it displaces, and which thus has to lift itself by aerodynamic means.

HEIGHT CLIMBER. The name given by the Germans to later airships designed during World I that were capable of climbing to altitudes above about 17,000 feet.

HELGOLAND. Small island off northwestern Germany in the North Sea, heavily fortified by the Germans during World War I and often used as a staging point for zeppelins heading off on raids against cities in England.

HELIUM. An inert, nonflammable gas used in airships and other lighter-than-air craft; the second lightest gas.

HELMSMAN. The individual assigned to steering an airship.

HIGH COMMAND. The highest order of joint command in the German military during World War I.

HORSEPOWER. A unit used to designate the power rating of airship motors and other engines; equivalent to 550 foot pounds per second or 745.7 watts.

HULL. In aeronautical usage, the major, cigar-shaped portion of an airship.

HYDROGEN. The lightest gas known and the only one used in German airships, despite the fact that it is flammable and explosive when mixed with even small portions of air.

INCENDIARY. A shell, bomb, or grenade containing a substance that burns with an intense heat when triggered by timing, impact, or other means.

INCLINOMETER (BUBBLE). An instrument used to indicate the upward or downward angle of an airship in flight.

KAISER. German for *emperor*, used in this book specifically to designate William II, Emperor of Germany and King of Prussia during the World War I years and grandson of Queen Victoria of England.

KAPITÄNLEUTNANT. A rank equivalent to that of lieutenant commander in the American navy, and the one to which most German airship captains were promoted.

KEEL. The lower, longitudinal girders of a rigid airship, used both as an essential element of the framework and, with a catwalk, as a corridor for moving from one part of the ship to another.

LEWIS GUN. A light, air-cooled, gas-operated machine gun with a circular magazine, first used in World War I. Named after its inventor, I.N. Lewis.

LIFTING POWER. The capacity of an airship to lift a given weight.

LIGHTER-THAN-AIR CRAFT. Airships, balloons, blimps, and any other craft capable of lifting into the air because they are lighter than the mass of air they displace. These craft are said to have aerostatic buoyancy.

LINE SQUALL. A squall advancing along a front that forms a more or less definite line.

LONGITUDINAL GIRDER. A very lightweight beam, usually constructed of aluminum or laminated wood, used as part of the framework of rigid airships and running the full or partial length of the ship.

LUFTSCHIFF. German *airship*.

MACHINIST'S MATE. An enlisted man in charge of operating or supervising the operation of an engine on a vessel or airship.

MAIDEN FLIGHT. First flight of an airship.

MAYBACH. An engine designed around 1910 especially for use in powering zeppelins, combining light weight, fuel economy, and reliability, and named after the engineer who designed it, Carl Maybach.

MIDLANDS. The central part of England, including a number of industrial cities, such as Birmingham and Leicester. A prime target, with London, for zeppelin raids.

MOORING. A pyramidal structure or strong mast used for the temporary holding of an airship in position outside its hangar or shed. The base usually rotated so the ship could be kept constantly headed into the wind.

MOORING MAST. Mooring.

MUNITIONS. Materials used in war, especially ammunition, weapons, and explosives.

NAVIGATOR. The individual assigned the responsibility for charting the path of a vessel or airship and keeping it on course through the use of instruments, radio communications, visual observation, and other means.

NONRIGID AIRSHIP. A lighter-than-air craft such as a balloon or blimp that does not have an internal or external framework and whose shape is maintained purely by the expansion of the gas or hot air inside it.

NORTH SEA. Arm of the Atlantic Ocean between Great Britain and the mainland of Europe over which all German airships flew in raids on England.

NOSE. The bow of an airship.

OBSERVER. Individual aboard an airship assigned the duty of observing the terrain, the weather, and any possible threatening enemy activity.

ORDNANCE. Machine guns, artillery, ammunition, and other military weapons or supplies.

ORTHOPHONE. Known popularly as "ears," mechanical acoustical devices designed by the British during World War I to detect the sound of aircraft engines.

PARACHUTE FLARE. *See* Flare.

PATROL ZONES. Zones assigned to British airplanes that searched out and attacked German airships raiding England.

PERISCOPE. An optical instrument, used particularly in submarines, for viewing objects above the level of direct sight.

PETROL. British term for *gasoline*.

PETTY OFFICER. A noncommissioned officer in the navy or airship service.

POMPOM. An automatic antiaircraft cannon invented prior to World War I.

PROPELLER. On airships, usually a two-bladed propeller made of very hard wood, sometimes with a veneer of a second wood, varnished.

RADIOMAN. The individual in charge of the radio or wireless aboard a naval vessel or airship.

RATE-OF-CLIMB INDICATOR. An instrument measuring the rate of ascent or descent of an airship or airplane.

RIGID AIRSHIP. An airship having a full inner skeleton or frame, as differentiated from nonrigid and semirigid craft.

ROYAL FLYING CORPS (RFC). The British military unit designated to build, maintain, and fly airplanes and train pilots and other personnel for flight and maintenance. Became part of the Royal Air Force on 1 April 1918.

RUDDER. The vertical fin or blade at the stern of an airship used to change the vessel's direction while in motion.

SAILMAKER. The individual on an airship assigned to maintaining and repairing the envelope, gas cells, and other fabrics.

SCHÜTTE-LANZ (SL). Designation of certain models of German airships similar to zeppelins manufactured by a competitor named for its two founders.

207

SCOUTING. Seeking out enemy aircraft for an attack.

SEARCHLIGHT. A large, powerful light on the ground used to detect enemy airships in the skies at night.

SEMIRIGID AIRSHIP. An airship that does not have an internal skeleton, but maintains its shape by means of a rigid keel and the pressure inside the gas bag(s).

SHED. *See* Hangar.

SKIN. *See* Cover.

SPEAKING TUBE. A tube used for conveying voices over a limited distance on a vessel or airship.

SPIN. An aircraft's vertical descent while spiraling, sometimes out of control.

STABILIZER. A horizontal or vertical fin on an airship or other aircraft used to keep it stable in flight.

STALL. The condition of an aircraft that has been caused to fly at an angle greater than the angle of maximum lift, thus causing loss of control and a downward spin.

STERN. The rear, or after, end of a vessel or airship.

STREAMLINING. Refers to the cigar-shaped airship hull and the design of gondolas, engine cars, and other exterior elements to slip through the air with the least possible air resistance and drag during flight.

TAIL GUNNER. A machine-gun operator stationed at a position in the rear of an airship or other aircraft.

TRACER. Ammunition used by fighter planes during attacks on airships. It contained a chemical substance causing bullets to trail smoke or fire to make the path visible and help the gunner to aim on a target.

TRIM. The capability to remain level and in balance when in flight or getting ready for flight.

TROLLEY. A wheeled device affixed to a track and used to hold adjustable guylines or wires when moving an airship into or out of its hangar.

TURBULENCE. Irregular movements of the atmosphere that cause gusts and lulls and make flight difficult for large aircraft such as zeppelins.

USEFUL LIFT. The lift of an airship after subtracting the weight of the ship itself and its various elements from the gross lift.

VALVE GAS. To open a valve in an airship or other lighter-than-air craft so that some of the buoyant gas is released, thus reducing or reversing the upward movement of the craft.

VERY PISTOL. A pistol designed by American inventor E.W. Very for shooting colored signal flares.

WEIGH OFF. Balance an airship so that it is floating in the air just above the ground and ballasted so the weight of the ship is distributed evenly.

WIRELESS. Any communications system, such as radio, that requires no wires or other connections between sending and receiving stations and is operated through the use of electromagnetic waves.

ZEPPELIN. Specifically, an airship produced by the Zeppelin works in Germany; any airship made from 1909 to the late 1930s.

Much of the original research for this book depended on materials and writings from the late Captain Hans von Schiller, with whom the author was in contact during the preparation of a number of articles on zeppelins some thirty years ago. Of special value was his 132-page unpublished autobiography, *A Million Miles in a Zeppelin*, which started with Schiller's experiences in zeppelins during World War I and traced his airship career during the immediate postwar period and his later operations into the mid-1930s, with particular focus on his command of the *Graf Zeppelin* on many memorable flights. He also provided clippings and photographs and prepared almost a hundred typed pages of comments, notes, quotes, and profiles of notable airshipmen he knew, including Captain Ernst Lehmann, Dr. Hugo Eckener, and Count Zeppelin himself. These were all used in the preparation of this history, as well as in the author's earlier articles on airships in war and peace.

The following books will be of interest to readers who may want to know more about zeppelins during World War I and the development and demise of airships during the peacetime years from late 1918 until the ultimate disaster, the crash of the *Hindenburg* in May 1937.

Ambers, Henry J. *The Dirigible and the Future*. Edelweiss Press, 1981.

Botting, Douglas. *The Giant Airships*. Alexandria, Virginia: Time-Life Books, 1980.

Bowen, Ezra. *Knights of the Air*. Alexandria, Virginia: Time-Life Books, 1980.

Bruce, J. M. *British Aeroplanes, 1914–18*. New York: Putnam, 1957.

Dick, Harold G. and Douglas Robinson. *The Golden Age of the Great Passenger Airships, Graf Zeppelin and Hindenburg*. Washington, D.C.: Smithsonian, 1985.

Eckener, Hugo. *My Zeppelins*. Ayer, 1979.

Gamble, C. F. *Snowdon: The Story of a North Sea Air Station*. London: Oxford University Press, 1928.

Hayward, Charles B. *Dirigible Balloons*. London: Shorey, n.d.

Hildebrandt, A. *Balloons and Airships*. Charles River Books, 1976.

Hook, Thomas. *The Shenandoah Saga: A Narrative History of the U.S. Navy's Pioneering Large Rigid Airships*. Airsho, 1981.

Jackson, Donald D. *The Aeronauts*. Alexandria, Virginia: Time-Life Books, 1980.

Keller, Charles L. and Douglas Robinson. *Up Ship! U.S. Navy Rigid Airships, 1919 to 1935*. Annapolis, Maryland: Naval Institute, 1982.

Lehmann, Ernst A. and Howard Mingos. *The Zeppelins.* J. H. Sears & Co., 1927.

Morison, Frank. *War on Great Cities.* London: Faber & Faber, 1937.

Raleigh, Walter and H. A. Jones. *The War in the Air.* London: Oxford University Press, 1922–1935. (Six volumes, of which III and V have maps and extensive accounts of zeppelin raids.)

Robinson, Douglas H. *Giants in the Sky: A History of the Rigid Airship.* Seattle: University of Washington, 1973.

Robinson, Douglas H. *The Zeppelin in Combat.* Seattle: University of Washington, 1971.

Smith, Richard K. *The Airships* Akron *and* Macon. Annapolis, Maryland: Naval Institute, 1965.

Toland, John. *The Great Dirigibles: Their Triumph and Disasters.* Peter Smith, n.d.

INDEX